DECEIT

Easton Zachary

EZ PUBLICATIONS OK

To all those looking for love

INTRODUCTION

It started with a match. A smile, a message, a promise. Online dating seemed like a simple way to connect. But behind one perfect profile was someone I never should have met.

This is not a love story. It's a warning. Because sometimes, the real danger isn't in meeting a stranger—it's trusting in one.

CHAPTER 1

Mason was getting tired of his day-to-day. It wasn't bad to be the only neurologist in his small rural area, but his life did get lonely. He took a deep breath and placed his hand on the cool metal doorknob to enter the treatment room. Plastering a smile on his face, he stepped in and greeted the young boy sitting on the exam table and his mother standing next to him.

"Morning, James," Mason closed the door behind him. He took a few steps to sit on the little rolling stool in front of the computer. Mason noticed that James looked nervous. Mason's smile became more genuine as he tried to comfort the kid. It was normal for a kid to be nervous coming into a specialist's office.

"Morning, Doc," James smiled halfheartedly and looked at his mom, who nodded approvingly.

"So, I hear you're in for migraines, is that right?" Mason looked between the mom and the kid. Usually, the moms of his patients felt inclined to speak for their kids; he wondered how it would be today.

"Yes, Dr. Santiago," James' mother leaned closer to her son and put a hand on his shoulder, "he's been struggling with migraines for about a year now." Mason wasn't hopeful this would go how he wanted, but he'd been proved wrong before.

"That sounds quite miserable, I'm sorry to hear it, James. Could you tell me about what happens with them?" Mason unlocked the computer and started typing out his assessment. He really hoped the mother would let her kid talk.

"Sure, they're behind my eye and just happen pretty randomly," James kicked his feet back and forth as he let them dangle.

"Ok, what else?" Mason began typing into his pre-filled-out form.

"They get really bad really quick, especially if I'm exposed to bright light."

"Uh-huh," Mason sucked on a tooth, his usual listening habit, and turned to look at James. "How long do they last?"

"Sometimes it's a few hours, but lately it's been days. I've missed school and swim practice a lot," the kid looked down, ashamed.

"James, do you get nasal congestion or sweating with these?" Mason grabbed his pen out of his pocket and fiddled with the clip on the end. James looked up, shocked.

"Yeah, how did you know?"

"And do your eyes swell and get red and runny?" Mason was glad to note that the mom wasn't running the show. He didn't need a Gypsy Rose fiasco on his hands.

James looked at his mom in surprise, then turned back to Mason. Bingo, Mason had hit the right spot.

"I thought I was just getting sick a lot from the migraines." James looked seriously shocked. Mason had seen the look before. It was a look of surprise that someone understood you.

"Tell me, when did your PCP, primary doctor, last do your migraine assessment?" Mason leaned forward, anticipating the answer before it was already given.

"About a year ago when I first started getting them." James

looked to his mom who nodded in agreement.

"Yes, that's right," she looked up hopefully at Mason.

"As I thought," Mason used the pen to scratch at a spot on his temple. It really was frustrating being the only person who understood these things sometimes. "Well, James, I don't think you have migraines. I think what you're experiencing are called cluster headaches."

"Cluster headaches? Aren't those supposed to be really bad?" James sat back, a confused look on his face. Mason could tell James didn't want to have something that was worse than what he had, not realizing that he had already suffered from the worst.

"Yes, they are. You would know best, actually," Mason gave a half-smile in sympathy. This poor kid had been going around with the wrong diagnosis for over a year. No wonder things weren't working out for him.

"There's no one at fault in these situations; it was just a missed diagnosis." Mason spent the rest of the session discussing treatment plans and reassuring the kid and his mother that they didn't do anything wrong.

After mother and son had spent a whole five minutes profusely thanking him, Mason excused himself from the room to go find his Medical Assistant, Sherry. Sherry was a squat but strong woman who always reminded him of a pit bull. Adorable from a distance but dangerous if you pushed her over the edge. "Hey, Sherry, James and his mom are ready for you. It was a misdiagnosis, the kid's got cluster headaches. Could you go over the next steps with him and have them follow up in a month?"

"Sure, Dr. Santiago," Sherry grabbed her clipboard, "I'm glad you caught this one. Imagine, that poor kid suffering for no reason!" Mason was glad to see the motherly side of Sherry peak through. With four kids of her own, the young woman was proud to care for every kid who came through the door like they were her own.

"I agree, and it's been the same PCP who's been doing the misdiagnosing. Maybe we should reach out to their office for an educational seminar on the different types of headaches? Could you remind me of that next week?" Mason stepped toward the door across the hall and pointed, eyebrows raised in question. Sherry nodded her approval.

"Sure, no problem. Yes, that's the one. You've got Mrs. Braverman next." Sherry smiled and headed into James' exam room.

Mason took a steadying breath to clear his mind for the next patient, Mrs. Braverman. He needed to stay on his toes with this patient.

"How's my favorite patient?" Mason grinned into the room and found the old woman there with her husband sitting on the exam table next to her.

"Oh, doctor, stop it," The seventy-year-old Mrs. Braverman blushed and waved him off. Her husband elbowed her in the side and glared at his wife of fifty years, but not unkindly.

"Six months since the stroke!" Mason whistled low, "That's no small feat. How are you feeling?"

"Better than ever, Doc, really!" Mrs. Braverman only slightly slurred, the right side of her mouth drooping just somewhat more than the left. It was a considerable improvement since Mason had first seen her.

"Well, your blood pressure, lab results, and MRIs are looking miles better. I'm really proud of the work you're doing! Are you still staying on the diet we talked about?"

Mr. Braverman's eyebrows went all the way up to his receding hairline.

"Grace won't let me eat a single cookie, doctor!" Mr. Braverman jokingly complained.

"Well, if I have to do it, you have to do it too, Joe!" Mrs. Braverman said in a mocking tone. Now, it was her turn to elbow him in the side. It was, in fact, Joe Braverman who had insisted on doing the diet together. He was determined to get his wife and himself back to tip-top shape. Joe had said he would do anything for the love of his life. It warmed Mason's heart. It stabbed his heart a little, too.

"We've been doing our tai-chi every other day, too," Mr. Braverman said proudly.

"I'm glad to hear it!" Mason leaned in conspiratorially, "Between you and me, a cookie won't hurt too bad every once in a while, but don't tell the doctor I said that." Mason straightened back up with a wink at the couple, who grinned broadly. He was so glad to see the two of them doing so well.

"OK, stick with the blood thinners, the tai-chi, the diet, and follow back up with me in another six months. Any questions?" Mason sat and patiently waited for them to answer. He hated for his patients to feel rushed.

"When can I come off the blood thinners?" Mrs. Braverman asked. His heart sank a little as he was waiting for this question. Mason hated to have to tell her this part. He knew how badly getting off these meds meant to her.

"Well, Grace, I'm sorry to tell you, but you'll have to be on these for the rest of your life if you want to avoid another stroke." Mason's mouth pulled into a slight frown.

Grace's face fell, and Joe wrapped his arm around her comfortingly.

"That's alright, babe! It's not too bad. If I could take it for you, you know I would!"

"I know, honey," Grace patted her husband's knee with her wrinkly hand. Mason's chest pinched at the sight.

"OK, any other questions?" Mason made sure to look them both in the face and smile encouragingly.

"None, Dr. Santiago," Mrs. Braverman said, a smile returning to her face.

"Then you are no longer my prisoners," he said with

another wink, "you're free to go!"

"Yippee!" Joe hopped off the table, still spry for his 70s, and helped his wife down. He handed her the cane she had recently graduated to. They walked arm-in-arm out the door and down the hall.

With a sigh, Mason headed back to his desk. He'd been the only neurologist in his small rural area in Nebraska for over a year. He'd initially joined the rural program to bring physicians way out here to the middle of nowhere as a financial incentive. It was nice to get away from the things at home as well. It didn't hurt that it was a change of pace from the bustling Chicago life, either. He'd worked in Glenview, the best suburb northwest of Chicago and loved every minute of it. However, he couldn't turn down the financial gain.

Peaking at his phone, Mason was anticipating a notification, but nothing popped up on his screen.

"Not still expecting her to call, are you?" Mason looked up to see Monica walking up to him. She was the Nurse Practitioner he shared a clinic space with, and he liked to think of her as his right-hand woman.

"Who me? Never!" Mason deflected. Monica was a middle-aged, tall, reedy woman with blonde hair and large-framed glasses. She was the most fashionable woman in this town. She didn't care what you thought of her, and Mason admired her for it, along with her wit and intelligence.

"Don't worry about her, Dr. Santiago. Like I said before, she's not worth your time." Monica sat on her desk next to his and wiggled her mouse.

"I know, but I can't help it," he gave what he hoped would be a winning smile. Monica rolled her eyes and tucked her head into her paperwork. He sighed, grateful that Monica dropped the subject.

Sighing again, he opened his computer to begin the tedious charting process before his next patient. Mason's

11

roster was filled with strokes and migraines for the day, but nothing too exciting.

Five o'clock rolled around just as it always did, and it was time to make the nearly hour-long commute back home. Mason wished he had more patients to see; he wasn't ready to head home yet.

"Any fun plans tonight, Mason?" Monica pulled off her white coat and began putting on her peacoat.

"Just a fluffy dog to hang out with. Would you want to grab a bite at Mungo's?" Mason asked hopefully.

"Can't, I've got plans with Josh. Maybe another time?" Monica grabbed her belongings and waved at him with her keys in hand.

"Yeah, see ya tomorrow," Mason waved and turned to Sherry, who was packing her things. "Sherry, you up for Mungo's?"

"Wish I could, Doc, I've got to pick up the kids from daycare. Shoot, I'm already late. Have a good night!" She rushed out the door, barely turning to look at him on her way out.

Mason haphazardly piled his belongings into his backpack, walked out the backdoor, and got into his truck. Turning the key in the ignition and pulling onto the main road, the vast plains expanded before him. Nausea roiled in his stomach, looking at that hour-long drive that awaited him.

The hour passed in drolls. He tried to ignore his phone while sitting in the passenger seat, taunting him with the lack of messages popping up on the little black screen. He tried to find a good song on the radio, but the turn of the hour only boasted ad after ad. Slamming the off button, he grumbled about the low quality of backcountry radio stations.

Finally, Prairie Point, the small town he called home, appeared on the horizon. His spirits lifted slightly as he turned into his neighborhood and pulled into his driveway. The small house was modest, but he was glad to have a place to call home. Turning off the truck, he reached over and glanced at his phone. Still nothing. At least he had Wasabi's smiling face to greet him when he opened the door.

"How's my best guy?" Mason opened his arms wide, and the mountain of fluff rushed into them to greet him with a happy "woof" and lots of cuddles. Wasabi was the husky he rescued from the pound the day after arriving in Prairie Point. "Did you have a rough day without me?" Wasabi whined. "It must be so terrible being here all by yourself all day. I'm sorry, pal. I wish I could take you to work with me, but you know I can't."

"Ruff," Wasabi nudged Mason's hand on top of Wasabi's head. It was his way of demanding scratches behind his ears. Mason couldn't help but laugh and obliged his furry friend.

The house oozed with quiet. The only sounds that could be heard in the house were Mason and Wasabi's footsteps across the hardwood floor and Wasabi's excited breaths. It was Wasabi's favorite time of day, dinner time.

The dropping kibble into the metal bowl ricocheted off the walls and vaulted ceiling. Wasabi hungrily attacked the bowl. Mason set to change out of his clinic and wear something more comfortable for a night filled with mindless scrolling on the internet.

He thought he felt his phone vibrate in his pocket. Quickly, he pulled it out and was resigned to find it was only a figment of his imagination. His phone seemed to laugh at him with its no messages. He chucked the phone onto the couch and set out to grab his fast-food leftovers from the night before. Mason was a terrible cook. Everything he touched turned to char, even with diligently following instructions.

The microwave beep echoed through the house. Mason grabbed his food and plopped in his recliner. He glanced at his phone again, face down on the couch. He huffed and began to eat the burger that was steaming on his lap. Switching on the nightly news, he couldn't help but wish that someone else was here to improve this mediocre evening.

After hours of mindlessly flipping through all his apps and no longer paying attention to what was on the TV, he gave up hope that she would text him.

"Alright, buddy, time for bed," Mason wiped his smooth hand down his face and shuffled off to his room. Plopping on his bed, he felt the shift as Wasabi cuddled up next to him. Mason grabbed his phone again and started watching lawn care videos. He fell asleep to the gentle snores of his dog matching the mowing sounds from his video.

CHAPTER 2

The morning came quietly, as it always did, slow and steady. The sky was as clear as day, and he knew it was going to be beautiful. Mason liked to get up early to go to the gym and start his day on the right foot. The near-empty gym was only occupied by the front desk girl and an old man who was always here at the same time Mason was.

The workouts were his daily meditations. He could focus solely on the movement and exertion of his muscles. Running was a drug, and lifting weights was an addiction. Mason poured himself into working out. It cleared his mind of anything and everything.

Before he realized it, the hour had passed, and it was time to get ready for work. Mason regretted that his precious hour was over. He scrolled mindlessly through his notifications on the way to the showers. He grunted in frustration; she still had not texted him.

The scalding water of the shower made him focus on the pain instead of anything else that might wander through his head. As he dressed, the mirror showed him his brown hair and eyes, which were nothing special. His average build grew stronger every day, just as he liked.

He felt nausea at the thought of the long drive. Thankfully, it subsided at the thought of a busy day filled with work. His schedule today was completely full, and he wanted to focus on helping as many people as possible. If he had it his way, he would expand his clinic hours and see even more people if he could. Slamming the locker shut, he left the gym, determined to conquer the day.

Stepping into the truck, he selected his morning 80s rock playlist and blasted the radio, getting lost in the music. Each new song indicated a different landmark (using landmark was putting it generously since there was not much out here). Each landmark told him how much longer he had left to get to the clinic, the last being a little, dilapidated shack on a corn farm.

The shack looked abandoned for the last twenty or more years. The corn farm around it looked to be well-kept. Mason had always wondered why the shack had been left by the wayside.

The last few minutes of his drive were filled with the music droning on in the background, but Mason's thoughts seemed stuck with the shack he was rapidly speeding away from. How could the farmers keep the corn field so well but give up on that shack? Was it of no more use, or was it just simply left to rot?

By the time he had pulled into the small town of Sandhill Creek, his imagination had taken him far and wide. He pulled into the parking spot and shook his head to clear it. It was time to focus on the day ahead.

As he stepped inside, the clinic was empty—it usually was this early in the morning. Mason liked to be the first to arrive, to let everyone know he was serious about his role and took pride in his job. He wanted everyone to know who was in charge here.

Just as he was setting down his bag, he heard the door open and looked to see Monica walking through. Today, she was dressed in high-waisted pants and a bold floral top. She looked great, as always.

"Morning, Monica, nice outfit," Mason complimented her with a smile.

"Thank you, sir, I picked it out myself," she retorted with a roll of her eyes and a faint smile. She had told him many times before that he didn't need to point out her outfit choices every day, but Mason couldn't help himself. He felt it was important for Monica to know her efforts weren't unnoticed, and he appreciated that his coworker took pride in her appearance.

"I'm about to get breakfast from Miss Susan. Would you care to join me?" Mason offered.

"Sure, that sounds lovely. I haven't seen her in a while!" Monica shouldered her bag, and they headed across the street to the hospital. The clinic and hospital had been here for thirty years, but they were both unusually small. The hospital only had about thirty beds but had a cafeteria for patients, staff, and family members that Mason tried to visit daily. He loved to see Miss Susan and her bright smiles and warm compliments. She had been a cook there since the hospital opened, and everyone loved her.

The day was unseasonably warm for November, but Mason wasn't complaining.

"So, did she text you?" Monica asked as they made their way through the parking lot.

"No," Mason answered briefly. How was your night with Josh?" Josh was Monica's long-term boyfriend, stationed at the nearby military base.

"It was great, thanks. So, when will you stop expecting this girl to contact you?" Monica asked with a raise of her eyebrows. Mason sighed; Monica wouldn't let him out of this one. He didn't want to talk about the woman who had broken his heart but didn't see a point in arguing with Monica about it. She got it out of him one way or another.

"I'm not sure. How do you think I should go about getting over her?" Mason grinned at Monica as he pulled open the door to the cafeteria, allowing her to pass through it before letting himself in after her. They continued walking down the hall.

"The same way you got over the last one, Mason. You know, you really can't put so much stock in these women. They always end up breaking your heart anyway." This was not the first time she had advised him so, but apparently, she wasn't yet tired of reminding him how stupid he was.

"I just can't help it," Mason replied, still smiling, hoping to soften her a bit, "I want to find somebody."

Monica said nothing but looked at him with the same piteous look he always got from her. The one that told him he was a blooming idiot. The look asked, "When will you ever learn?"

"I know, I know," Mason scratched the back of his head. They stepped into the cafeteria and formed a short line for Miss Susan's window.

"I know that online dating used to work for you in Chicago, but maybe it's just not the same out here?" Monica stepped forward in the line.

"You're probably right. I just can't help but hope that she'll be out there the right one." Mason didn't want to talk about this anymore, so he deflected back to Monica again, "So what did you and Josh do last night?"

"We did a sip and paint night. Josh is terrible with a paintbrush, but it was a lot of fun! We should go with all the clinic staff and their spouses sometime!"

"That sounds like a great idea!" Mason genuinely loved the idea. However, he wished he had someone to take, as everyone else would definitely bring their spouses. Mason hated showing up to these alone. A man of his status shouldn't be showing up stag. He took a deep breath and sighed through his nose as he waited for the person in front of them to order.

"Everything alright?" Monica asked inquisitively.

"Yeah, just fine," Mason lied and smiled brightly. She didn't need to know what was going through his head. She would just lecture him again.

Spared from further questions, it was their turn. They stepped up to the window, smiling at Miss Susan. Miss Susan was in her 60s with wiry gray hair and a matching wiry frame. She looked like a gust of wind would blow her over at any minute.

"Morning, dears!" Miss Susan called over the counter, "What can I get for you today? The usual for you, Mason?"

"Yes, please, Miss Susan. How ever did you know?" Miss Susan smiled, got Monica's order, and started cooking.

"How's the morning, beautiful?" Mason winked at the elderly woman, and she blushed.

"Oh, Dr. Santiago, I'm doing just great! Couldn't complain, you know. I've gotten to serve the lovely people of our hospital, and I feel just so blessed to do so." The woman was so genuine it made Mason look away quickly

He couldn't understand how Miss Susan was so happy with her life. It always astounded him that a simple job could be so rewarding. He would rather pluck out all his eyelashes than work as a cook.

"So, do you think we should do it in the next two weeks or next month?"

"Do what?" Mason had seemed to lose track of the conversation.

"The clinic sip and paint night!" Monica looked at him as if he had hit his head.

"Oh, yeah, let's do it in the next two weeks. Right before Thanksgiving will be good. And then the Christmas party can be our event for next month." The two providers liked to do something with the staff at least once a month to promote a good working environment and work-life balance.

"That's what I was thinking, too. We'll have to check with Steven just to be sure," Monica's eyes gleamed with the joke. Steven was their clinic's manager. He was a balding, middle-aged man who was never present in the office. He managed all seven of the hospital's clinics, and because he was always busy, he rarely had time to come in. Steven always signed off on whatever the providers wanted to do for the staff. However, he was a stickler to the rules. The manager's biggest goal was earning as much profit as possible from their healthcare system.

"Oh, that will be a tough one, alright," laughed Mason.

"Here you are, dears! Have a blessed day and stay out of trouble!" Miss Susan grinned broadly. The two beamed back at her and promised to do so. Mason paid for Monica's breakfast, ignoring her cries of protest, and they headed back toward the clinic.

"You can pay for me next time, then, woman, jeesh. Can't allow me a little courtesy of spoiling my fabulous coworker?" Mason nudged her with his elbow.

"Oh, cut it out," Monica huffed, and they set off for the clinic. Mason couldn't tell what was bothering her. He thought she would be delighted to have her breakfast paid for, but he guessed wrong. They stepped outside, and he noticed the horizon had become full of stormy rain clouds.

"Full day for you?" Mason tried to veer the conversation to something a little more manageable that wouldn't upset Monica.

"Yes. I've got at least four new emergency cases I couldn't fit in yesterday. Our caseload is getting quite heavy. I think it's about time I ask Steven to hire another provider."

"Do you think he'll agree to that? You've been doing a good job carrying on by yourself," Mason knew immediately that Steven would never go for it. Hiring another provider would be the last thing on his mind. Steven had just gotten rid of the receptionist for Mason and made her work the load between the two clinics.

The receptionist, Ashley, had been Mason's favorite. She was his right-hand woman for a whole six months before she left. She never complained about listening to him and always gave sound advice he could follow. Ashley also never whined when Mason wanted to spoil her. He hadn't gotten over the loss yet and couldn't quite find it in himself to forgive Steven.

"I hope so. I feel like I'm drowning," Monica looked stressed.

Mason couldn't relate to Monica's feelings. He loved being busy with work—the more, the merrier, in his opinion. The parking lot was filling up with more cars, and Mason was glad the day was going to start soon.

"You're doing great!" He encouraged, "Hang in there." They had arrived back at the clinic. Monica didn't say anything in reply. They ate their breakfast silently at their desks as they looked over their prepped charts for the day. Sherry, the receptionist, and Monica's Medical Assistant filtered in through the door to start the day. Mason greeted them with his winning smile and welcomed his first patient, who Sherry had just roomed.

Mason didn't notice that his phone had dinged with a new notification from the dating site.

CHAPTER 3

The clinic walls were blurring as Mason seemed to fly from room to room. The business of the day had prevented him from taking a break. He felt adrenaline like he hadn't felt it since the days of working on a call in the ER in Chicago. It filled him with joy to be so busy.

His mouth was filled with "take care of yourselves," "I'm so glad I can help," and "I'm so sorry" throughout the whole day. He and Sherry were in perfect time with each other. Their flow state seemed to overtake the office, too. Liking the effect he had on the clinic, his smile grew wider with each patient. Mason couldn't help but feel he was winning this day.

Finally, at five o'clock, he had sat down to chart. The pile of paperwork told him he would be here late tonight, which suited him just fine. The only problem was Wasabi. Mason picked up his phone to text his neighbor, Greg, to ask him to take Wasabi out and feed him.

Greg was a police officer who worked the night shift and lived next door to Mason. Mason did the mental math. Greg would be leaving for work soon. If he got ahold of him now, Greg would have enough time to take care of Wasabi.

Ignoring his notification-filled screen, he sent a quick

message to Greg, who instantly replied, "No problem!" Mason was glad that he could count on Greg.

Then, curiosity nipped at his brain, and he couldn't help but look at the notifications even though he had a lot of work to do. There were texts from his ex-wife, Christine, telling him that the house they sold was finally all wrapped up and she didn't need anything further from him. Typical spam messages from apps he barely looked at filled the screen, too.

His breath caught when he saw a notification from Elite Pursuit, the dating website for men of means and status to find elevated women. He'd been using the site for several years now with relative ease. The most success he found was in Chicago. Nebraska had no success so far, but he was ever hopeful.

Clicking open the app, he saw a message from the most stunning woman he'd ever laid eyes on.

"Hi, handsome! I know it may be bold, but I saw your profile picture, and I just got the best feeling about messaging you!" The message seemed to pulse in front of his eyes.

Am I dreaming?

Mason decided to wait to respond until he got home. He tried to focus on his work, but he kept thinking about the dark-haired, blue-eyed woman he had just seen on his phone. She was literally perfect in every way. Other than her ears, she had no piercings. There were no noticeable tattoos, either. Her body was, well, incredible. Mason tried in vain to focus on his charting, but visions of her popped into his head.

"Everything ok, Dr. Santiago?" Mason jerked his head up to see Sherry standing over him.

"What?" Mason was panting, and he couldn't figure out why.

"Is everything alright? You seem to have wandered off

somewhere, and you're breathing really heavy." Sherry's concerned face told him he clearly looked weird. He cleared his throat.

"Yes, just fine! Sorry!"

Sherry raised her eyebrows and walked over to her desk; the look on her face said she didn't believe him but didn't want to push it. He was grateful she left him alone. Wanting to not be distracted, he tucked his head into his work. However, the thoughts of the woman kept spilling into his head. He just realized that he hadn't even read her name.

Looking up at the clock on the wall, he saw that two hours had passed since he started. He felt like he barely got any work done. Unhappy with his focus levels, he decided to call it quits for a day.

Avoiding touching his phone, he packed up his things and headed straight out the door. Mason hadn't even realized everyone else had gone home for the day.

Sliding into the truck's front seat, he tapped open Elite Pursuit and stared at his message again. Diane. Her name was Diane. She looked to be about twenty-five or so. Mason couldn't help but think how perfect she was. Her eyes seemed to welcome him in. He looked at the message again and pondered hard over what to say to her.

The clouds ahead opened, and the rain came down upon his windshield. Tap. Tap. Tap. The rain pounded on the truck until he couldn't think straight.

Huffing, he turned the truck on and decided to think about it. He didn't want to spoil whatever this could be. The whole ride home, he thought of what he might say to Diane. He had already envisioned a future with her. Taking her to fancy dates, jetting off to Miami for the weekend, or visiting his old stomping grounds in Chicago. She was his perfect match; he just knew it.

The rain poured down on the truck the whole way home. For the first time in months, he listened to nothing on his commute home. He hadn't listened to his own thoughts since he couldn't remember when.

CHAPTER 4

Dr. S.: Hey, beautiful lady. I'm glad you decided to be bold. How are you this fine evening?

Mason had gathered his courage and finally figured out what he wanted to say. He hit "send" before he had time to fully process what was happening. Wasabi was glad to have him home and he was glad to be back in the comfort of his own house. Mason hated being at clinic when he got messages from dating sites. The last few times had ended so poorly, he didn't have the heart to tell everyone there was another girl again. He was also a way from curious eyes.

Diane: I'm doing just splendid, thanks! Your profile says you're a doctor, that's amazing! How long have you been a doctor?

Dr. S.: Thank you. About twenty years.

Diane: That's amazing. It's so cool that you can care for people like that!

Dr. S.: Thanks. What do you do for work?

Diane: Oh, I'm between jobs right now. I'm hoping to open my own beauty salon soon, though.

Dr. S.: That's great! So, tell me about yourself.

Diane: Well, I'm an only child, but I have a lot of cousins.

My mom died and I'm super close with my dad. I've been doing hair for about five years. I love getting to take care of people in my own way. What about you?

Dr. S.: I'm divorced with two kids who don't want to see me much. I live alone with my dog, Wasabi. Wasabi is a husky puppy and I just adore him. He's my best friend. I've been a doctor in town for about a year now and I absolutely love it. It's nice to not be on-call. I moved from Chicago where I was practically a hospitalist, which is not what I do. My specialty demands respect, so I left to find somewhere that respects me.

Diane: Wow, that must be hard to have kids who don't want to see you much. And a dog! I love huskies, they're adorable! Can I see a picture of Wasabi? And I totally understand needing to find somewhere that respects you. On a much smaller level, I did the same thing. I'm nowhere near as important as a doctor, but I agree with you. It's important to be where you're wanted. How great that you got to find someplace that appreciates you and your talent.

Mason could hardly think straight. This woman understood him. He couldn't believe it. They'd been talking for only a little while, but she understood his desire to be respected and appreciated. He could never get this kind of treatment from his ex-wife. The other girls he'd spoken to had never quite gotten it like Diane did. Not as quick as she did anyway.

He didn't even want to think about the last girl, the one that Monica teased him about ruthlessly. That was just embarrassing, and he didn't want to think on her while this perfect creature was here for him now.

It helped that she lived on the other side of the state. It wasn't necessarily close, but he was happy to drive a few hours to see the right person.

Diane: Tell me about your favorite things.

Mason: Well, I'm obsessed with pizza. There's

surprisingly a lot of good pizza joints here in Nebraska.

Diane: No way, me too! I love the pizza places here in my area are great too!

Mason: Maybe we should go on a tour of all the places someday.

Diane: I would love to! That sounds great!

The night went on with Diane and he talking about everything and nothing. She liked almost all the same things he did. He was happy to tell her about his stories as a doctor, and she shared some of the worst haircuts she'd ever seen. Diane made him laugh in ways that he couldn't describe.

He felt a stirring in his heart that he didn't expect to feel again. Already, he wanted to meet this girl. He couldn't stop thinking about how perfect in every way that she was.

Diane: What do you do for fun?

Dr. S.: Honestly, there's not much to do for fun around here. It's tough living in the middle of nowhere. Also, before I do anything fun, I feel like I need to wait. I want to do those things with a future significant other. I don't want to waste my time doing them by myself when I could be making special memories with someone special. Does that make sense?

Diane: I totally understand that. It's very romantic, really.

Dr. S.: You think?

Diane: Definitely. It shows that you're soft-hearted and thoughtful.

Dr. S.: So, you don't think it makes me sound pathetic?

Diane: Not at all! I think it seems very understandable. It's important to do things with someone special.

Dr. S.: I'm so glad you understand. I thought I'd come off as a weirdo or something.

Diane: Not at all. <3

Dr. S.: Well, if it's not too forward, I'd be very happy if you and I could go do something fun together sometime.

Diane: Not too forward at all! I'd love to!

Dr. S.: Would this weekend be too soon?

Diane: This weekend would be perfect!

The rest of the evening was spent making plans for the upcoming Saturday for them to meet half-way between her town and his. It would be an hour and a half long drive, but he knew it would fly by. That night, Mason fell asleep dreaming of pizza tours with a dark-haired beauty.

CHAPTER 5

The next day Mason was full to bursting with excitement for his upcoming weekend plans. The sun shone brightly all throughout his morning routine, Wasabi was extra cuddly, and the time seemed to fly by on his commute. He even felt like he could lift more weights than he normally did. The shack stood at the edge of the journey looking slightly happier than it did before. He couldn't quite put his finger on it, but it made him happy to see.

Stepping into the clinic, he was surprised to see Monica there. Was he late? He glanced at his watch to find he was there at the usual time.

"Morning, what are you doing here so early?" He wasn't sure why it irked him that Monica was there before him.

"Oh, hi, Dr. S. I just had a few charts I didn't get to last night, so I came in this morning to finish them off before my first patient. I don't want to get behind." Monica looked slightly frazzled. Mason couldn't fault her for wanting to stay on top of her work.

"Ah, gotcha, well, it's good to see you. Busy night?" Mason put on his most winning smile.

"Just dinner plans with the family, they're in town for the

rest of the weekend," Monica smiled back at him.

"Family is definitely important. I'm glad you got to see them." Mason set all his stuff down on his desk and started prepping his charts.

"Me too. We went to that new pizza place on First Street. I highly recommend, it's even better than Mario's."

"Better than Mario's, no way!" Mason grinned as he batted his hand in the air as if to fend off her very clearly wrong answer.

"It really is, I swear!" Monica laughed.

"I'll believe it when I see it," Mason teased but then his tone shifted to one of more seriousness, "but I'm glad you get to spend time with your family. I know how much you've missed them lately." Monica's face fell into a half smile. He got the reaction he wanted, gratitude that he remembered and is thinking of her.

"Thanks, Mason," Monica put a hand up to her heart and then cleared her throat, "What did you get up to last night?"

Mason debated telling her the truth. Should he tell her of yet another girl he'd been talking to online? After the disaster that was the last girl, he wasn't sure how much teasing he could take from the clinic. Ah, screw it. This girl could be the one.

"I started talking to a woman online," Mason grinned widely. Monica's eyebrows rose.

"Really? What's she like?" Her eyebrows still hadn't gone down

"She's warm and funny, smart and kind, very personable. She's a hairdresser." Mason's heart started to beat a little faster. Why was it beating faster?

"Yeah? What's her name?" Her eyebrows were still glued in place. He expected her to notice how bright and bubbly he'd been today. Slowly her eyebrows lowered, no longer showing her blatant questioning and doubt.

"Diane," he started grinning again, hoping she'd catch on to how much he liked this girl

"Diane, that's pretty!" Monica turned back to her computer.

"What is it?" Mason leaned forward. Why wasn't Monica more excited about this?

"It's nothing, Dr. S., I'm happy for you." Was Monica jealous? No, she couldn't be.

"Seriously, what's up?"

"I just think that you should be careful. Maybe take a break from the online dating and focus on yourself for a while?" Mason jerked back as if slapped.

Mason was stunned. Monica had never talked to him this way before. Sure, she'd given hints that she was wary of the girls before. He'd always told her about his online dating, but never had she spoken to him like this before. Mason wasn't sure what to do. He didn't want to offend Monica, but it wasn't really her place to be telling him what to do.

"Thanks for your honesty," Mason said shortly and turned to his computer. He just wanted to focus on the day so he could get one step closer to meeting Diane.

Monica winced. "It was just a suggestion, doctor... I only say that because I know how hard you work to please these women and they don't seem to give you a lot in return, but if you like this girl and she's good for you, then I'll support you."

Mason sighed and turned back to Monica.

"Thank you, I appreciate it. She really is amazing, Monica. I think you'd really like her." Mason tried to give his most reassuring grin.

"I bet I would," Monica smiled gently back and turned back to her computer.

Mason felt a sense of irritation. Why did she have to ruin his perfect day? Couldn't Monica just be happy for him? Sighing again, he turned to his own computer and started the work for the day.

An hour later Sherry came in. He put on a smile for her and greeted her like he always did.

"You seem cheery this morning, doc," Sherry said.

"Thank you! I am! I started talking to a new girl." Mason couldn't help but laugh.

"That's great! Tell me about her!"

There, see, was that so hard? That was the reaction he was hoping for. He proceeded to tell Sherry how wonderful Diane was and how excited he was to meet her for their date this weekend. He was thrilled to see Sherry excited for him and still irked that Monica didn't have the same reaction.

Once Sherry was on her way for the morning he huffed, determined to not let Monica's sour mood ruin his joy. He had a big weekend ahead of him he needed to prepare for. The phone in his pocket dinged and he pulled out to see a message from Diane.

Diane: Thinking about you this morning, handsome. Hope your day is going well!

Dr. S.: Better now that I'm talking to you!

He spent the rest of the day talking to Diane in between appointments. The staff could tell he was distracted, he knew, but didn't care. Let them see how happy he was. He couldn't wait to show them all how wonderful this was going to be.

CHAPTER 6

Saturday morning rolled around, and Mason was bubbling with joy and anticipation. Wasabi received extra cuddles in the morning, and they went on a particularly long walk through the neighborhood. The sky was piercingly blue, the birds were singing, and he hoped his joy could seep into others.

He had been talking to Diane the whole week, and she truly did seem like she could be the one he could spend the rest of his days with. They had started sharing their deepest desires and silly wishes. They'd messaged nonstop the last few days. She was the first person he spoke to in the morning and the last person he talked to at night.

Was he being a little reckless with how fast they were going? Maybe, but Diane was worth it. Building up the courage he required to go see a stranger was the easiest task in the world. Mason felt like he could take on an entire football team in a fight. Was he a little nervous? Sure, who wouldn't be nervous after meeting the potential love of their life?

The drive to the midway point was excruciatingly long and only five minutes at the same time. It was strange how an hour-and-a-half drive could turn you into a messy ball of energy. He passed many corn fields and farms that were quite empty of all signs of life.

What felt like a lifetime later, he arrived at the pizza place where they said they'd meet for lunch. It was called Guacamole Joe's, a silly little play on the fact that it wasn't a Mexican restaurant but a pizza spot. The building was a brick pizza joint, and he chuffed at the joke of the name.

Mason sat in his truck and waited for his phone to ring or to see a sight of Diane. He considered going inside, but it was early, and he didn't think she'd be there yet. A minute went by, and his heart started to beat heavily. Was he really going to do this? Five minutes and his heart rate picked up. What if she didn't like him in person? Mason huffed. That was impossible. Everyone liked him.

Ten minutes had passed, and he checked his phone. No message or call from Diane. Now was the time they said they would meet, so he should just relax. Twenty minutes went by. The tension in the truck was palpable. Was she bailing on him?

Twenty minutes after they were supposed to meet, there was still nothing. Did someone stop her on the road? Was she kidnapped? His thoughts started to spiral. The people outside kept passing by his truck, and he still couldn't see her. Mason contemplated walking into the restaurant to see if she was inside. Then his phone buzzed.

He rushed to look at the screen and sent the phone flying across the truck to the passenger side floor. Scrambling to get over the center console, he was jerked back and choked by his seatbelt. Swearing, he unchecked the darn thing and practically threw himself onto the passenger side. The center console punched him in the gut, and he lost his breath for a second. He coughed and wheezed to get his breath back. His arms were outstretched to the floor, and he felt the phone slip through his fingers several times before he finally got a firm grasp on it. He really needed to get himself together.

The phone screen lit up, and on it, he saw a message from

Diane. He finally caught his breath and gasped. Swiping open the screen, his heart pounding now, he read the words that would change his world forever.

Diane: I'm so sorry to do this to you, but I have to cancel.

Dr. S.: Oh, wow. I just got here. I'm sorry to hear that you have to cancel. I'm rather disappointed to hear you aren't coming, to be honest. Is everything ok?

Diane: I just found out that my father died.

CHAPTER 7

TEN YEARS EARLIER

Mason sat in a dingy hospital room on a very uncomfortable chair. The fluorescent lighting was giving him the start of a migraine. The room smelled of bodily fluids and cleaning chemicals, which wasn't pleasant. However, he wanted to be here for the man lying in the hospital bed next to Mason.

It had been ten excruciating days of sitting in this room since Mason first got the call from the hospital. Grateful that he was a physician, he was able to understand the process, but it was still hard to wrap his head around the fact that his dad was the person who had a stroke.

Now, ten days later, he was sitting at the death bed of his father. The stroke was so massive that it impeded his father's ability to lift his limbs, and he was barely able to lift his head off the bed. What little speech his father had left was slurred and mushy. Quite frankly, his father sounded like a golden retriever, and it was impossible to understand almost everything he said.

Mason had spent the last week and a half attending to his father's needs and being the caregiver. He wouldn't allow anyone except him and the hospital staff to do it. If it were up to Mason, he'd be the one to do all of the work. Still, the hospital would not let him diagnose, prescribe, and administer medication. Mason wanted his family to see how dedicated he was to his father. His aunts had been in to visit daily, but his sister never bothered to show.

He would show them all that not only was he capable of taking care of his father, but he was proud to do so, and they should be proud of him too.

Steven violently coughed from the bed for a few minutes. It was grating on the ears, but it must have been more miserable to be in the bed. Steven's color went from grey to blue, and it worried Mason; was this the time? Developing hospital-acquired pneumonia was another blow to the already devastating stroke.

Mason leaned forward and helped suction his dad's mouth. Once the coughing subsided, Mason gave his water. Steven mumbled something incoherent.

"I know, Dad, I know. Just rest," Mason patted his father's arm and tucked him back into the covers.

Steven looked as deeply into his son's face as he could, and Mason felt his father's weighted gaze.

Muffled, his father spoke slowly and clearly, "Son. I love you."

CHAPTER 8

Dr. S.: Diane, I'm so sorry. Do you need anything?

Diane: I don't know what I need right now. I'm so confused.

Dr. S.: Of course, it's totally normal to be shocked. Can I help you with anything?

Diane: Not right now but thank you. I just need some space. I'm sorry you drove all that way, and I couldn't be there.

Dr. S.: Please, don't even worry about it. Just focus on you and your family now. If you need to talk, I'm here for you.

Diane: Thank you. I'll let you know.

Mason sat in his truck bewildered. Her father was dead. He felt the hit so deeply. He remembered sitting at his father's own deathbed.

Turning on the truck, he sighed as he faced the long drive home. He was so disappointed not to meet the love of his life today. Why did these things always happen to him?

The ride home was fraught with frustration. He reviewed various scenarios about what he would have done if he had been there with her. He imagined comforting Diane at her father's bedside and holding her while she sobbed. Mason imagined them coming together in love and grief to create beautiful moments together. He would plan the funeral with her; she would be so grateful to him for his help, and they would spend their days healing together.

Hours later, he pulled into his driveway and sighed. Fully accepting that this would end the relationship and the end of the dream of Diane, he turned off the ignition and slammed the door shut behind him. At least he had Wasabi with him.

Unfortunately, there was no food in the house. Mason wasn't much of a cook and hadn't planned to eat here tonight. The thought of having to find food for himself made him angry as he furiously tapped on the screen of his phone to order a pizza. If he couldn't celebrate the start of a new beginning with her, he could at least have some pizza like he was anticipating.

While waiting for the pizza, Mason hopped in the shower and let the hot water beat down his back as the steam filled the bathroom. When finished, he stared at himself for a long time in the foggy mirror. He tried to make out his features through the steam but couldn't. He went to the bedroom and pulled on a beat-up t-shirt and some old shorts.

"What a waste of time," Mason grumbled to himself as he trod down the silent hall into the kitchen to feed Wasabi. "What an absolutely ridiculous waste of time. That's it, I'm done."

The doorbell rang, and he opened it to find a pimply teenage boy carrying his order. Mason grabbed his wallet to tip the delivery boy.

"Can I offer you a piece of advice, kid?" Mason didn't know what had gotten into him, but he needed to share his newfound misery.

"Uh, sure, sir," the pizza boy was hesitant.

"Don't fall in love," Mason sighed, grabbing the pizza and passing over a generous tip.

"Uh, ok, sir," the pizza delivery boy's eyebrows came together in confusion and suspicion. He gave a look that said,

"What a weird dude," and he took the money and almost ran back to his car.

Mason spent the evening scrolling through meaningless videos. Wasabi was extra needy for attention, which grated on Mason's nerves more than he could handle. The dog would whine by the back door, and Mason would get up to let him out, but Wasabi never went outside. He just proceeded to whine.

"I'm not going out there, dog. You can, though," Mason shut the door and returned to his recliner and pizza.

Five minutes later, Wasabi was whining again. Mason stood up and opened the door to let the dog out, to no avail. Five more times, this happened, and Mason's thread snapped.

"What do you want, dog?!" Mason bellowed at the thing who scampered off to the bedroom. An angry sigh escaped his lips before he said, "Well, fine! If that's how you want to be!"

Throwing himself into the chair, he grumbled about the stupidness of animals. Not long after, Wasabi came up meekly and put his nose on Mason's toes.

"Come to your senses, have you?" Mason reached out a hand and scratched his dog behind the ear. Wasabi's tongue lolled out as he sat patiently by his owner's side until the man fell asleep with an extra piece of pizza in the box. Wasabi sneakily grabbed the last piece, scarfed it down, then laid down and fell asleep by Mason's chair.

———

At two AM, Mason jolted awake so hard that the front legs of the recliner lifted off the floor, and he nearly flipped the recliner backward. Wasabi lifted his head off his paws from the floor and jumped up when the chair slammed back down to the ground.

"That was a close one, huh, boy?" Mason's heart was racing, and he reached down to feel the velvety fur of his dog.

Wasabi licked his hand and then stretched before trotting off toward the bedroom, groaning for Mason to follow him.

"Alright, alright, you silly beast. I'm coming." Mason padded after his dog but realized he left his phone on the chair. Turning to grab it, he saw that his phone lit up for a second, then went dark again. It was unusual for the hospital to need him. He was seldom on-call, but they needed him for an emergency case at the ER every once in a blue moon. It's why he kept his phone on to alerts and never had it on "do not disturb."

Tapping the screen to get it to light up again, he saw that it wasn't the hospital that had messaged him. It was Diane. He could barely make out the "Hey, I'm..." from two hours earlier before his phone died.

Swearing under his breath, he quickly went to his room and plugged the phone into the charger.

"Come on, come on, hurry up!" Mason begged and demanded the phone. What felt like an eternity later, the phone glowed back to life. He typed in his passcode and opened the app to see her message. The system was slow as it was still loading, and he cursed short battery lifespans.

Finally, he opened her message, and his heart raised a little.

Diane: Hey, I'm so sorry to blow you off. I feel terrible. Hopefully, we can meet up someday after all this craziness.

Mason released a breath of relief. Was there still hope? He typed out his message and hit send.

Dr. S.: Hi, I'm so glad you messaged me. Please don't be sorry. I completely understand. How are you doing?

Chewing on his inner cheek, he wondered if she'd still be awake. He climbed into bed and pulled Wasabi close, waiting to see if she'd reply. Then, the tiny dots appeared at the bottom of the screen to indicate that she was typing. His heart started pounding.

Diane: Thank you for understanding. It's so hard to do anything right now. Having your support means more than you know. I'm ok. I've been trying to process my grief while figuring out logistics. I need to get to Washington, D.C. by tomorrow to plan the funeral and get my dad's affairs in order.

Dr. S.: I'm sure that can be overwhelming. I'm glad to be here to support you. Whatever you need, ok, Diane?

Diane: That is so kind of you, doctor. Really, you have no idea how much it means to me.

Dr. S.: Of course, I'm here for you.

Diane: Do you really mean that?

Dr. S.: Absolutely.

Diane: ok, well....

Dr. S.: What is it?

Dr. S.: Is everything ok?

Diane: Well, no. It's so embarrassing to have to ask you this. I normally never ask for help on anything. I'm a very independent person who works hard for what I need, but....

Dr. S.: But?

Diane: Well, I need help. You know how you said you'd do anything for me? Well, I really need some money to get to Washington D.C... I don't get paid for another week, and I don't have enough money for the plane ticket right now.

Dr. S.: I can totally understand that. How much do you need?

Diane: The ticket is $350. I know it's so much money, and believe me, I wouldn't ask unless I absolutely had to, but I just bought some supplies for my hair salon business, and they aren't refundable. I won't be able to pay for it myself until next week, but my dad's lawyer needs to meet with me as soon as possible.

Dr. S.: Ok, well, I can lend you the money, no problem. Just pay me back when you can, ok?

Diane: Really? Thank you thank you thank you! I don't

know what to say. I'm so grateful for you, doctor. You're a real lifesaver. You really have saved me from this problem. Ugh, I'm so grateful for you, I could cry. Actually, I am crying. Can you believe that?

Dr. S.: You're welcome, my dear. Please know that you deserve this, ok? Stop crying. How can I get this money to you?

Diane: Well, do you have ZapFunds? That would be the easiest way.

Mason looked at his phone for a long minute, breathing in and out slowly. Was this another one? He'd been hurt before by someone only wanting money out of him.

Diane: Dr. S.?

Diane: You ok?

Could he do this again? He scratched the back of his head, disturbing Wasabi from his peaceful slumber. Wasabi groaned at him and went right back to sleep.

Dr. S.: Yeah, I'm alright. I just needed to think about this for a second. I've been hurt by a woman before who was just scamming me. You're not doing that, right?

Diane: Dr. S., that's a big accusation to make! I wouldn't scam you! Right after the death of my father and you accuse me of scamming you? I'm sorry you were hurt before, but that's no reason to distrust me. I'm sorry but screw the woman who hurt you before. I'm not like that. I'm different, I swear.

Dr. S.: Ok, I believe you. I just don't want to be hurt again.

Diane: I'm so sorry you've been hurt. That's insane that someone would take advantage of you like that.

Dr. S.: Yeah, thanks.

Diane: I promise I will never hurt you like that. To be quite honest, I've been holding back something from you. Something I think that you should know.

Dr. S.: What is it? Are you ok?

Diane: Oh, yeah, I'm alright considering the situation. I just wanted to let you know something really important. Promise you won't get mad or go crazy.

Dr. S.: Yeah, ok, I promise.

Diane: Well, I've been thinking about our time together and how wonderful it is to talk to you. I don't even know your name, but I feel so drawn to you and cared for by you. You're interesting and kind and intelligent and funny. I... I'm in love with you.

CHAPTER 9

*A*round nine, he woke up to Wasabi whining and pawing him in the face.

"Oh, hang on, boy, hold on. We'll get you there!" Mason and Wasabi raced to the back door so he could let the dog out. The chill morning air blasted him in the face the second he opened the door. It refreshed Mason wide awake despite the limited hours of sleep. Leaving the door open just wide enough for Wasabi to slip through, Mason got ready for his day.

For a moment, he almost forgot about why he was so tired. Then, it hit him. After hours of talking with Diane into the wee hours of the morning, Mason couldn't stop smiling. Thankfully, he didn't have to work, so he spent the day napping, eating, and texting Diane.

He thought back to last night. How his heart skyrocketed. Had he read those words, right? Did she really say that? Could she finally be admitting to herself what he's known about how he feels about her all along?

The Night Before

Dr. S.: You might not believe me, but I'm in love with you too.

Diane: Really? Oh, honey, I'm so excited to hear it. I can't believe it.

Mason was grinning from ear to ear. He couldn't fathom how lucky he was. He and Diane stayed up all night talking about their plans. She repeatedly told him how in love she was with him. That he was the sun and the moon, and she was the stars in the sky. The reality of it hit him like a brick being thrown at his gut. He was in love. He had found the one.

With that reality in front of him, sending her the money she needed was easy, and he did so willingly. Her gratitude knew no end, and he felt like a hero.

Dr. S.: Tell me about your dreams...

Diane: Well, I want to come home to you. I want to spend my life loving you and getting to know you every day. I want us to be happy and to have a lot of dogs and travel.

Dr. S.: Yes, we'll be the power couple of all the other couples. People will wish they could be like us.

Diane: Exactly! A power couple. I like that. You're so smart.

Dr. S.: Well, I'm not a doctor for nothing haha.

Diane: Smart and funny. Aren't I a lucky girl?

Dr. S.: Yes, you are. And I'm a lucky man.

Diane: You really are, Dr. S. Oh! Another dream I have is to get out of my crappy apartment. My roommate is nice and all, but I want something nicer and bigger. This place is so tiny, and the landlord doesn't care about us at all.

Dr. S.: Well, how about you move in with me?

Diane: What?? Are you serious?!

Dr. S.: Why not? I own the house after all. It would be good for you to get out of your dingy place.

Mason sent her photos of the house. It was definitely a bachelor's house.

Diane: Oh, honey, I love it! It looks amazing! I would love to live with you! How about when I get back from the funeral stuff, we can talk about me coming?

Dr. S.: I would love nothing more.

The Next Day

The oven timer beeped five hours later, saying his pizza was ready. He spent the whole day talking with Diane. He set the phone on the counter, put on the gloves, pulled the oven door open, and was about to pull the pizza out when another message from Diane appeared. Mason stood there shocked, the heat radiating from the oven and the beeping continually going, harmonizing with the ring in his ears. Wasabi whined at him a couple minutes later because he still hadn't moved.

Blinking back his shock, he slammed his finger on the "timer off" button, grabbed the pizza out of the oven, and slammed the door. He dropped the pizza on the top of the stove. Ripping his gloves off, he looked at his phone with trepidation.

Diane: Honey, I have to ask you something. I know it's crazy and way too soon, but I don't know what else to do. I've been asking everyone else around me, and they've given what they could, but I don't want to be a burden on anyone, especially not you. Would it be ok if I borrowed some more money for getting around and stuff while I'm in D.C.? I know it's crazy to ask you this. Believe me, I wouldn't if I didn't have to, but I have nowhere else to turn. My cousin gave me all the money he could, which was only $100. I won't get paid until next Friday. I promise I'll pay you back as soon as I can. I'll be in D.C. in a few hours, and then I have to plan this funeral and get my dad's affairs in order. The lawyer keeps changing the appointment times and stuff. I'm afraid I won't be able to eat while I'm there. I don't know what else to do.

Mason's fingers quickly pounded out a response.

Dr. S.: Of course you can, my dear. I'm nervous that you feel like you have to beg! Why do you think I wouldn't give it to you? I'm here for you, whatever you need. Pay me back when you can. How much money do you need?

Diane: Oh my god, I'm crying with relief. Thank you so much, honey. I thought you would hate me for asking. I'll need $300 at most, I promise. Just this once.

Dr. S.: Don't forget, I've already given you money, honey. I'm happy to do it now. Just make sure you're taken care of. I need you to eat and take care of yourself so you can come to me when all this craziness is over.

Diane: I promise I will. Thank you for supporting me. I'm really going to need your emotional support these next few days. This will be so hard. I'm so grateful for you and glad I found you.

Dr. S.: Of course, I'm here to support you in any way you need. You're my person, Diane.

Diane: You're my person too, Dr. S... By the way, what is your first name?

Dr. S.: Oh, I thought you knew it. It's Mason.

Diane: Mason, I love it. It's a perfect name for a perfect man.

Mason tossed a pepperoni over to Wasabi and sat down at the kitchen table for the first time in a long time. Sending the money over, he imagined having Diane sitting across from him. He got lost in daydreams of her decorating the place and adding her feminine touch to everything. Diane would be happy to get out of her dingy apartment, and she would be happy being his partner.

Framing up Wasabi in his phone camera, he took an adorable picture and sent it to Diane.

Dr. S.: Wasabi says: Can't wait for mommy to come home and live with me!

Diane: Oh, my goodness! My Wasabi, I can't wait to live with you! I'll be the best mommy to you, ever. I promise! I'm going to make you and your daddy very happy.

CHAPTER 10

"What do you mean she's going to live with you?" Monica stood in shock in front of Mason the next Monday he worked.

"Just exactly that! Isn't it great?" Mason was beaming. He felt like he could kiss the sky.

"It's something…," Monica raised her eyebrows and put her hands in her white coat pocket. The clinic was unusually busy for a Monday. He didn't have much time to chat with her, but he couldn't wait to tell her the good news. However, this wasn't the reaction he was hoping for.

"What do you mean by something?"

"I just mean," Monica sighed, "isn't this a little fast? You haven't even met her yet."

"But when you know, you know, Monica." He pulled open a chart and started examining the contents.

"How do you know? Again, you haven't met the woman," Monica's lips pursed incredulously, and her eyebrows managed to rise even higher. It was all emphasized by the crossing of her arms. That was the end of it for him. Mason wouldn't let Monica speak poorly of his love like that and ruin his mood.

"You just don't get it, Mon. She's great. You'll see!" Mason folded the chart back together and turned when Sherry called for him

"Dr. S., Olivia is ready for you in room 3." Sherry, leaning on the wall, inclined her head toward the exam room. "I know we don't have a pediatric neurologist, but you're the best bet we've got." Hearing Sherry's confidence to deal with the four-year-old with numbness in her fingers was exactly what he needed to brush off Monica's bad mood. She'd understand eventually once she met Diana.

"I'll be right there, Sherry!" Mason smiled at his assistant, who ran to her next task. He turned back to Monica. "Look, I understand it's new-"

"And you've fallen for scams like this before," Monica pointed out.

"Yes, you're right, but this one is different, I promise. Diana's smart, kind, and witty. She loves Wasabi. As soon as she's back from her father's funeral, she'll move in, and everything will be perfect. You'll see." He purposefully called out the funeral part to get the NP to back down a little bit.

"Oh, I didn't realize her father had died. Why didn't you tell me?" Monica looked frustrated.

"Well, it wasn't exactly fun to mention, and I hadn't gotten the chance yet." Mason shrugged.

"Dr. Santiago, don't forget room 3!" Sherry called out as she flitted from room to room.

"Be right there! Come on, Mon. Be happy for me at least," he said, taking a step toward the exam room.

"I-," Monica was interrupted by her phone ringing.

"I'll talk to you later this afternoon," Mason waved a hand and walked into the room to see Olivia and her father.

"Hello, Miss Olivia. How are you today?" Mason put on a bright smile as he entered the room. He found a man and a little girl sitting on the chairs next to the computer, with her sitting in his lap. Mason's heart melted. He knelt in front of the little girl to show her he wasn't all that scary. Olivia looked to her father to see if it was ok to talk to the doctor. The man nodded and gave her a squeeze.

"I'm... I'm ok. My hands... I can't feel them sometimes, and they sometimes hurt. I drop things a lot, too." Olivia was a brown-eyed, blonde-haired little girl. She was gripping a stuffed elephant.

"I'm sorry, my friend. That doesn't sound fun. What's your elephant's name?"

"Lawrence, we call him Larry for short." Olivia was gripping onto him with her arms, and her fingers flexed in and out as if she had lost grip strength occasionally.

"Larry is an excellent name. I wish I would have thought of that for my dog." He gave her a big smile, hoping the topic of animals would calm her nerves.

"What's your doggie's name?" Olive asked, peeking out from behind Larry's head.

"Wasabi. I love sushi." Mason whispered as if sushi were his guilty pleasure. He reached out and gave Larry a scratch behind the ear.

"That's a funny name." Olive giggled.

"It is, and he's a funny puppy." Mason peeked at her posture and noted she had a slight tilt to one side of her head.

"Olivia, can your daddy hold onto Larry for a second while I take a look at you?" Olivia nodded and bravely handed her stuffy to her dad and stood up. Mason had her go through the range of motion of her arms, legs, and neck. He noticed the deficits in her range and smiled reassuringly at the little girl. Behind her, the father silently watched with bated breath.

Mason picked her up and put her on the exam table.

"Ok, friend. I'm going to bring my friend Sherry in with me, ok?" Olivia nodded.

Mason peeked out the door to call Sherry in, who was

patiently waiting outside. Mason hated this part.

"Dad, can you tell me, has she had any potty accidents lately?"

"Yes, doctor. She feels very upset by them since she's been potty trained for a couple years now. She's also been dropping things and complaining of arm and hand pain." Olivia cuddled into her dad and hid her face in Larry's soft fur.

"Did anything happen like a fall? Is she safe at home?" Mason hated this part. It was never fun asking a parent this.

"Oh yes, very safe. Please take a look at her and look at it for yourself. I swear Olivia's mother and I have never laid a hand on her. She's a typical kid who bumps her head and plays with her sisters, but never is she in real danger!" The father's eyes were wide with fear, but they also held an understanding that this was a necessary question.

"Ok, sir, thank you," Mason said kindly and then turned to the little girl. "Can I take a look at you under your shirt and pants, sweetheart? Your daddy and Miss Sherry will be here the whole time, ok? Tell me if anything hurts." Olivia nodded again, and Mason started a full exam. The little girl looked safe and sound, and nothing hurt to the touch - not a bruise on her.

"Very good, friend." Mason finished the exam, and Sherry helped her get dressed. Once they were done, Mason held out his hand for a high-five, and the little girl shyly gave him one before heading back to her dad.

"You sure she didn't have any falls or accidents?" Mason waited patiently. Sometimes, it took asking a couple of times for patients to remember. The little girl's father looked contemplative, as if he were looking back through his memories.

"You know, she did fall down the bottom slide of the playground a couple of weeks ago. It didn't seem like an issue because she wasn't crying or hurt; it just startled her for a second. She landed on her back on the slide's edge but then bounced right up. There wasn't a bruise or scrape on her back afterward." Mason nodded, understanding.

"Olivia, do you remember falling on the slide?"

"Nope! But I fall down a lot sometimes, and it doesn't hurt! Momma says I'm still learning how to walk," she spouted off like any four-year-old, repeating what she'd heard her mother say. Mason smiled. She was a typical little kid.

"I think she has an issue with her spinal cord. If she landed the wrong way, it could have pinched something or done some damage. I'll need an MRI to be certain. Now, I know it can be scary for little ones to get MRIs, so we'll get anesthesiology involved so it can be as easy as possible for her."

Mason and the father discussed the next steps while Sherry played with the little girl. Once the dad's questions were satisfied, Mason and Sherry showed them out the door and waved goodbye to Olivia.

"That poor kid!" Sherry looked sadly down the hall after the girl.

"Absolutely. Just being a normal kid comes with risks. I'm glad her parents brought her in. Hopefully, we can get her the treatment she needs."

"You're an excellent physician, Doc." Sherry nudged him with her elbow and placed her hand on the doorknob to the next room, where a fifty-year-old woman with migraines was waiting. "This one is just a follow-up; it won't take more than a few minutes."

"Wait, Mason!" Monica called as she walked down the hall, a concerned look on her face.

"Sorry, I've got another patient waiting. I'll catch up with you after clinic, ok?" Monica sighed and turned down the hall.

"Wait, are you ok, or is it just the thing we discussed earlier?" Mason wanted to make sure he wasn't missing something actually important.

"Just the thing we were talking of," Monica gave a half

smile and headed back to her desk. Mason shook his head.

"She worries too much," he said to Sherry.

"She's concerned for a friend, sir. I think she's allowed to be worried. You would be if she were in your shoes, wouldn't you?" Sherry looked pointedly at him with her eyebrows raised.

"I guess, but she has nothing to be worried about. I'm happy, and I just wish she could be happy for me."

"If you say so, Doc," Sherry gave a mock salute and walked into the room, Mason trailing behind her.

———

When the last patient finally left, he was ready for a giant hamburger. He hadn't been able to eat lunch, and he was starving. Monica exited the last exam room. She removed her gloves and tossed them into the trash.

"Wiping down the room again?" Mason asked, but he couldn't believe how much she had given to the clinic, and she didn't have to.

"Yup!" Monica said with a half-smile. She looked exhausted.

"You know you don't have to do that. That's the cleaning crew's job," Mason pointed out.

"It's no trouble," Monica shrugged. Mason couldn't believe her.

"Do you have plans with Josh tonight?" Mason hoped they could grab some food, ease Monica's fears, and just hang out as friends.

"Nope, he's at the base all night. Wanna head to Mungo's?" She suggested.

"You bet, my treat. Meet you there, or want to drive together?"

"Since you're paying, I'll drive." Monica jingled their keys, and they left toward the car.

The drive there was filled with conversation about their cases of the day. Monica had a patient who stuck kick up their nose and another one who had put baby grapes down their ears. Of course, they were two-year-old twins. Mason had a ninety-year-old who wanted to make sure his memory issues were normal; they were. Monica had a follow-up on a burn patient who had rescued kittens from a fire. Mason had a heartbreaking case of early-onset Alzheimer's as a forty-year-old. They laughed and talked about the drama of the clinic. Mason was grateful to have a friend like Monica, who was intelligent enough to understand his daily struggles.

Once seated at Mungo's, their usual waitress, Betty, came to the table. Mungo's was a lovely place that served brunch all day, every day. It was actually nice food; Mason was surprised to find it in the middle of nowhere. It reminded him of a place that would be in Chicago. The environment was warm and welcoming, and the decorations were something you'd find on an Instagram feed.

"What'll it be today, you two?" she snapped her gum. Betty was an ancient woman who still dressed like it was 1952. Today, her curly gray hair was in a ponytail, and she wore a literal poodle skirt with an actual poodle patch ironed onto it.

"I'm starving for a giant hamburger today, Betty. Nice skirt, by the way," Mason gave the elderly woman a wink. She rolled her eyes at him.

"And for you, toots?" Betty looked at Monica. For some reason, Betty liked Monica more than Mason, and he couldn't figure out why. He'd always been kind to her and gently flirted with her to make her feel special. Never once had she shown any sign of liking Mason. He took it as a personal challenge to win the old woman over.

"I'll have the eggs benedict, please. Thanks, Betty," Monica smiled and handed their menus over. Betty smiled warmly at Monica and then turned away.

"That woman hates me," Mason fake whined.

"She does not. She just has no tolerance for your flirting," Monica said encouragingly.

"It's hopeless. The woman of my dreams and I, never destined to be." Mason pretended to gaze longingly after the waitress.

"I heard that, punk!" Betty called as she passed by their booth and dropped off two glasses of white wine. "This is because I know Monica had a rough day and has nothing whatsoever to do with you, doctor." She narrowed her eyes and pursed her lips at him as if to say, "Don't think anything otherwise."

"Thank you, darling!" Mason called after her. She waved her hand in dismissal with another eye roll as she walked away.

"Ok, maybe she does hate you," Monica laughed after Betty entered the kitchen. Mason dramatically gripped his chest as if his heart hurt and hung his head in feigned disappointment. They both cracked up.

Monica took a sip of the wine and sighed in relief before saying, "Ok, so tell me, how did it come about that you and Diane are going to move in together?" Mason stared at her in the face, assessing what Monica was trying to get at. She held her cards close to her chest. Mason decided honesty was the best way to go here.

"We've been talking every day. Diane's been really stressed with her father's funeral, so I figured I could try and help her with the burden by chatting with her. I'm crazy about her. I mean, have you seen how beautiful she is?"

"Actually, no, you haven't told me very much about her," Monica took another sip of her wine. Mason smacked his forehead. How had he not shown her Diane's picture yet? Monica would totally understand once she saw her. He pulled out his phone and flipped to the photos he and Diane sent.

There were the daily photos he sent her of Wasabi, his house, his drive to work, and his food. Diane had just sent a few photos of herself; some were meant for his eyes only. Finally, he came across the selfie he was looking for. He passed the phone to Monica.

Monica's face was priceless. It was everything he had hoped for. Monica looked back and forth from the phone to Mason's face.

"This is her?" She said slowly.

"I know, right?" Mason was practically dancing in his seat with giddiness.

"But this is really Diane?" Monica seemed confused.

"It is! Isn't it wonderful? She's the most beautiful woman I've ever seen!" Mason took the phone back and stared at her photo again. He couldn't believe how lucky he was. He looked back at Monica, who looked skeptical. "What?"

"It's nothing," Monica fiddled with her fork. Was she jealous?

"Seriously, what is it?" Mason was confused.

"I just... Doesn't it seem too good to be true?" Monica looked up hesitantly, afraid of his response.

"I know, that's exactly how I feel!"

"No, I mean, she's too beautiful, too perfect, Mason. Please don't take this the wrong way, but... Are you sure she's a real person?"

Mason's face dropped. He couldn't believe his ears.

"Of course, she's a real person-" he was interrupted by the arrival of their food. Betty smiled at Monica and snapped her gum at Mason. That woman was starting to get on his nerves. Once Betty left, he said, "What do you mean, is she a real person?"

"I just think that, like I said, it's too good to be true. That woman looks like a social media model." Mason sat back and crossed his arms.

"Wow, I didn't take you for someone who would be so judgey of other women. I'm surprised at you, Monica." He looked down the wine glass at her as he took a big gulp.

"It's not that," she held her hands out in supplication and then took another sip of wine. She cleared her throat and took a deep breath before saying, "I'm not meaning anything judgmental; I promise. I'm just trying to look out for you. We live in the middle of nowhere, Nebraska. People like that tend to move to LA or New York, you know? I'm just worried this is another scam. Another person trying to take advantage of you. I don't want you to go through what happened last time."

Five months prior, Mason had been scammed by someone on a social media site. It was a guy pretending to be a girl, and he'd given him a couple hundred dollars, thinking it was a poor soul in need. It was humiliating, and Monica had been there with him every step of the way. She was also with him when the last girl he met on a dating site had disappeared entirely and still hadn't texted him.

"You've got it all wrong. Diane's not like that. She's way better than the other girls. Or girl and guy, for that matter." Mason tucked into his burger. He didn't want hunger to get in the way of this conversation. He was determined to prove Monica wrong and couldn't do it on an empty stomach. Monica started on her eggs benedict.

"How do you know?" She said after swallowing her first bite.

"I just do!" Mason laughed incredulously. Monica chewed on her food slowly. They sat there in awkward silence while they both ate. After he could feel the hunger dissipating and his burger was half gone, he changed tactics, "Listen, Mon. I appreciate your concern; I really do. However, she's different. The last person never offered to meet me. Also, I looked up the space she wants to use for her salon."

"Ok, well, couldn't anyone just offer to meet you

somewhere? And couldn't anyone look up an empty space and say they want to rent it?"

"Fair, but I don't doubt her. I believe with my whole heart this is the right person."

"Wait, why did you say she wanted to use it for her salon? What happened?"

"Well, we agreed she'd need a place here in town if she moves in with me."

"Ok... then, how did it come about that you are going to move in together?"

"We were talking about how much better Sandhill Creek is than her town-"

"Sorry, what is her town?"

"It's a little thing called Medford in Eastern Nebraska. It's like three to four hours east of Prairie Point."

"I've lived here all my life and never heard of a Medford, Nebraska, Mason." Monica frowned.

"She says it's a really tiny town that's not very popular," Mason waved off, "Anyway, she was saying she's worried that the salon she wants to open won't be super popular since it's a small town close to Medford. We were also talking about how much it would suck to have to drive three to four hours, maybe more, if I'm leaving from Prairie Point just to see the woman I love."

"Wait, you love her?" Monica's mouth hung agape.

"Yes," Mason stared at her like he couldn't believe she was surprised by this. He made it pretty obvious. Mason finished the last bite of his burger, relishing every bit.

"The woman you started talking to like a week ago online? You're in love with her?" Monica's tone said she didn't believe it.

"Absolutely! And she loves me too. I mean, I wouldn't send money to someone I don't love, especially not after last time." Mason smiled broadly. Monica reached to take another sip of wine but realized it was gone. Right at that moment, Betty came up and refilled her glass.

"The wine's on the house, honey," she winked at Monica and turned without saying a word or even glancing at Mason. He really couldn't figure that woman out.

Monica took a long and slow sip of her wine. He looked down to see she had barely touched her plate.

"Mon, are you ok?" He was worried she was stressed about something at home. She and Josh had been together for seven years, and he still hadn't proposed. Mason always wondered if Monica was ok with it; she seemed to let on that she was not. Maybe she was jealous of Mason's commitment to Diane? That things were moving fast for him, and it wasn't for her? "Everything with Josh ok?"

Monica scoffed, "I can't believe you're asking me about the quality of my relationship when you are in this mess..."

"I'm not in a mess, Monica!" He tried to reassure her. He finished his wine and held it up in the air to signal Betty he needed a refill. He was going to take advantage of this being on the house. Monica said nothing as Betty refilled his glass and headed off.

"I assure you; you are. At the very least, it's strange." Monica pushed away her glass and crossed her arms.

"You mean it's strange to want to move in and spend my life with the woman I love?" Mason's blood started to boil. He took another sip of his wine.

"I mean, it's strange that you're doing this again. It's strange that you're falling in love with someone you don't know, willing to give beyond what is normal and sane for most people to do, and you're blind, Mason." They sat in uncomfortable silence. Mason kept drinking from his wine and debated his next words.

"That's funny, coming from someone who is blind to her own relationship." Mason cut back. Monica's mouth snapped shut. He looked into his glass; it was empty again. Betty came and refilled it.

"What's that supposed to mean?" She glared at him.

"I mean, isn't it strange that the man you've dedicated your life to, the man you have stayed in this tiny town for, hasn't shown some form of commitment?" He took another drink of wine.

"My relationship is not what we're talking about right now. And last I checked, I didn't open a conversation for you to examine my decisions. You were the one who wanted me to know about Diane. You wanted my opinion on her." Monica started organizing her area. Clearly, she was ready to go, but he wasn't done yet.

"No, I think it was you who was asking me about Josh. You always tell me how he's always gone, and it's disappointing. You always complain that he's still in the military and that you're stuck here because of it. Isn't that asking me for my opinion on your relationship?" He downed the rest of his glass.

"No, actually. That was me telling a coworker about my situation. I never asked for your opinion on what Josh and I have. My relationship is mine, not yours to judge." Mason couldn't believe how she was acting.

"I can't believe you're being defensive right now. I think you're misremembering. Wouldn't I, a neurologist, remember better than a Nurse Practitioner?" He hoped she would realize how ridiculous she was being.

"That is enough. I'm done having this conversation with you." Monica stood up to leave. She threw down some cash for her half. He was shocked she didn't see things his way.

"I said I would pay for it," Mason was flabbergasted.

"Don't bother," she shot back. "I hope you and Diane are very happy together, Mason. I really hope so, but when she breaks your heart, don't say I didn't warn you." She turned to leave.

"How am I supposed to get home? You're just going to abandon me?" He could tell he hit a nerve, but she kept walking away. She waved to Betty and let the door's bell jingle behind her.

Mason swore under his breath and gave his black card to Betty, who looked disgusted by him.

"Thanks, doll," he smiled charmingly at Betty, who ran his card through the mobile device.

"Don't call me doll, doctor. I'm three times your age, and I could still kick your ass to Sri Lanka." Betty handed him his receipt and turned away from him. He left her a very generous tip just to prove he was a decent guy.

On his half an hour walk back to the clinic, he thought over their conversation over and over again. Each time it played out, it left to one conclusion. Monica was jealous of him and Diane's love. She wanted a romantic whirlwind of her own and couldn't stand to see him happy.

CHAPTER 11

When he got home, Mason sat at his computer desk, the glow from the screen casting a soft light over the cluttered surface. His eyes were fixed on the chat window, waiting for Diane's reply. He ran a hand through his hair, anxiety gnawing at him. He'd been looking forward to their conversation all day, but there was a growing pit in his stomach he couldn't ignore. It worried him that he'd been waiting ten minutes longer than when they said they'd talk today. Was she ok?

Finally, the message popped up, and his worries deflated.

Diane: Hey doctor, how was your day?

Mason smiled, his fingers flying across the keyboard as he typed his response.

Dr. S.: It was ok. Better now that I'm talking to you. How about you?

Diane replied almost immediately.

Diane: Miss you so much

Dr. S.: I know, honey. I miss you too. I can't wait to hold you in my arms. How are you really, though?

Diane: I can't wait to be in your arms. Things have been tough. Trying to get my father's messy affairs in order is

DECEIT

exhausting, and I can't wait to leave this place. The house sale still isn't going through, and the lawyer isn't very kind. I wish I could be with you right now.

Dr. S.: I miss you too, Diane. Just hang in there. Soon, you'll be here, and we can start our life together. You'll never believe what happened to me today.

Diane: What, honey?

Dr. S.: The Nurse Practitioner I work with, Monica, is jealous of our relationship.

Diane: Well, she should be. We're amazing together.

Dr. S.: We are!

Diane: I just wish I could be there in person to show her she should be jealous. I don't like the idea of you working with a jealous woman. Is she pretty?

Dr. S.: She's nowhere near as beautiful as you, trust me. And believe me, I'm not attracted to her at all. She's got an ugly personality to boot.

Diane: I just wish I could be there with you. This whole thing is a disaster.

Dr. S.: Just a little while longer, honey. Then, we can make the whole world jealous of our love.

Diane: You're right, baby... But there's something I need to talk to you about. It's important.

Mason's heart skipped a beat. Not again...

Dr. S.: What is it?

There was a brief pause before the next message appeared.

Diane: Mason, I hate to say this, but there's been another problem. The lawyer is demanding his fee, and if I don't pay, I'll lose him. I need another $1,500. Please, love, I don't know what to do.

Mason frowned, his fingers hesitating over the keyboard.

Dr. S.: Can't you tell him to take it out of the house sale? Isn't that how this usually works? Didn't your father pay him

66

beforehand?

Diane: My father paid for his services then, not now. Mr. Buford also said that he couldn't take his fee out of the house sale. It doesn't work like that here in D.C. I guess...

He stared at the screen, torn between his growing doubts and deep feelings for Diane. He couldn't believe that he was letting Monica get to him, and it made him angry. He could almost hear Diane's voice and see her pleading eyes. He wanted to believe her and be her knight in shining armor. He typed slowly:

Dr. S.: Alright. I'll send it to you. But this has to be the last time, Diane. I can't keep doing this.

Diane: Thank you, Mason! You're my hero. I promise this is it. Soon, we'll be together, and all of this will be behind us.

Mason let out a long sigh and opened his banking app. As he completed the transfer, he couldn't shake the nagging feeling that something was off. But he pushed it aside, convincing himself that Diane was worth it. She had to be.

Mason and Diane spent the night discussing their future and exchanging words of love so sweet that it would make Monica sick to her stomach. He knew their love could change the world.

CHAPTER 12

Weeks later, Mason paced nervously in his living room, glancing out the window every few seconds. He had finally worked up the courage to talk to Greg, his next-door neighbor and closest friend besides Monica. Mason couldn't ignore any longer that he had sent far more money to Diane than he had ever meant to. He couldn't help it. The woman he loved needed help, and when the requests came in once a week, it was easy to support her. However, it was growing concerning that she still wasn't back when she promised to be two weeks ago.

Greg was someone Mason had always looked up to. They'd shared beers on the weekends, and casual conversations in their driveways, but this was different. Greg had been out of town on a training trip the last few weeks, but he got back last night. Mason needed to tell Greg about Diane, and he wasn't sure how to start.

Taking a deep breath, Mason stepped out of his house and walked the few steps to Greg's door. He knocked, the sound echoing loudly in the neighborhood. A moment later, the door opened, and Greg stood there, filling up the doorframe with his tall, broad figure. Greg had a small towel thrown over his shoulder. Clearly, he'd been working on something on his house. His red hair was wet from sweat, his green eyes wide, and a look of surprise on his face.

"Mason, hey," Greg said, smiling. "What's up? Everything ok?"

"Uh, yeah, can I talk to you for a minute?" Mason asked, his voice shaky. "It's important."

Greg's smile faded, replaced by a look of concern. "Sure, come on in."

Mason followed Greg into his house, a place that was both familiar and comforting. It was a small two-bedroom but comfortable. It clearly was a bachelor pad. Greg's fiancé, Amri, was away in New York getting trained at Parsons in fragrances. She had been there for six months and would be gone another six more months. Mason couldn't understand it but chalked it up to womanly wiles. He sat down at the kitchen table, and Greg leaned forward, his eyes searching Mason's face.

"How was your trip?' Mason didn't quite know how to tell Greg the truth, so he avoided it a little longer.

"It was great. I was stoked to see Amri. She's killing it at school. She'll make a great perfumer."

"Cool. And how was training?" Mason fiddled with his fingers.

"It was sick, man. Quantico is the place to be. I learned so much." The man looked happier than Mawson had ever seen him.

"That's awesome!" Mason smiled broadly, but he could tell it didn't reach his eyes.

"What's going on, Mason? You look like you've seen a ghost." Greg's face was kind and concerned.

Mason took a deep breath, trying to steady his nerves. "It's about someone I've been talking to online. Her name is Diane."

Greg raised an eyebrow, "Diane? Is she a friend, or...?"

"She's my girlfriend," Mason said, the words tumbling out quickly. "Well, more than that, actually. I'm in love with her. We've been talking for a few weeks now, almost a month. We met on an online dating site."

Greg's expression softened a bit, but there was a hint of skepticism in his eyes. "You've never mentioned her before. Have you met her in person?"

Mason shook his head. "No, we haven't met in person yet. She's been in D.C. for her dad's funeral and getting his affairs in order, but she's planning to come back soon." He took another deep breath, "When she comes back, she's going to move in with me." Mason congratulated himself silently for telling Greg the best news of Mason's life.

"Wow, that's fast, Mason. How are you feeling?" Greg's apprehensive face wasn't comforting Mason.

"Thrilled, honestly, but a little nervous," Mason rubbed a hand down his face.

"Ok," Greg said slowly, "so what's the issue?"

Mason hesitated, feeling a lump in his throat. He couldn't talk to Monica like this. He knew he needed to tell someone; he just didn't want Greg to judge him for it. "I've been sending her money, Greg. A lot of money. She said she needed help with travel expenses and other things. Monica thinks it's a scam, but I don't want to believe that."

Greg's eyes widened slightly, and he leaned back in his chair. "Mason, how much money are we talking about?"

"Thousands," Mason admitted, his voice barely above a whisper. "I know it sounds crazy, but I love her. I believe in her."

Greg ran a hand through his hair, clearly troubled. "Mason, I'm going to be straight with you. As a cop, I've seen this kind of thing too many times. People get emotionally invested in someone they've never met, and they get taken for everything they have. It happens more often than you think. Don't you remember last time?

"I know, I know," Mason said quickly. "But Diane's different. She's sent me pictures; we talk all day. It feels real. It is real!"

Greg sighed, leaning forward again. "Pictures can be faked, and people are easily manipulated. I'm not saying Diane isn't real, but you need to be careful. Have you ever tried to video call with her or talk to her on the phone?"

Mason shook his head. "She's always had an excuse. Bad internet, phone is broken, something always comes up."

"That's a red flag, Mason," Greg said gently. "If she really cares about you, she'd find a way to see you face-to-face, even if it's just over FaceTime."

Mason looked down at his hands, feeling a mix of shame and desperation. "I don't know what to do, Greg. I want to believe in her, but I'm starting to doubt everything. Monica told me this would happen, and I don't want to believe she's right. I can't believe she's right. Diane cares for me, man. I love her. She loves me. I know she does."

Greg reached across the table, placing a hand on Mason's arm. "I'm glad you came to me, Mason. The first step is recognizing that something might be wrong. Even if you and she love each other, there can be issues. Amri and I love each other, and we still struggle occasionally after a couple years." Greg's face clearly conveyed that he didn't believe Diane was real, but Mason appreciated him trying. "Let me help you, Mason. We can look into this together and see if we can find out more about Diane. If she's real, she'll understand your concerns and work with you to prove it."

Mason shook his head, "I don't know, man. What would that entail?"

"Well, for starters, I'll need all your communication and every photo she's sent you," Greg said, rubbing his hand on the back of his neck. He looked up to the ceiling for answers.

"I couldn't do that! It would be breaking her trust!" Mason

stood up quickly, his heart pounding.

"Mason, I don't mean to offend you, but how do you know that this woman is trustworthy in the first place?" Greg's hands were held out in supplication.

"I just do! You don't know her, Greg!" Mason stormed into the living room. He couldn't believe this was happening again. Would no one believe him? He needed to tell Diane how ridiculous this was.

Greg followed him into the living room, "Ok, fair, but do you know her?"

"See, this is what I was afraid of. I knew you would blame me for this!" Mason's blood was boiling. He needed to talk to Diane. She would understand him.

"I'm not blaming you for anything, man. This could happen to anyone!"

"What? Finding love with someone in need? Being happy with someone who is actually willing to come to where I am instead of making me go to them? Have you told Amri that you don't want to move to New York?"

Greg looked hurt. Good. He needed to feel what Mason was feeling. "No, I haven't told her. But this trip showed me that I won't mind it. I'm happy to be where she is!"

"Sure, you are! You're happy to just give up your own life here, is that it? I can't believe you would lecture me when you have your own issues to work out. I'll see you later. You'll see when she gets here." Mason stormed out the door and slammed it behind him.

When he got home, he told Diane everything. He needed someone who understood him, someone who would support him without judgment. Diane was the only person who ever did that.

Diane: He's just jealous, Mason. He won't understand because his fiancé wants to change him. I don't want to change you. He'll see when I get there. I love you so much and I can't wait to show you how much and prove everyone wrong.

Mason was thrilled she felt the same way as him. He barely minded when another request from Diane came for $250. He sent it smiling, reassuring himself that his love would soon be here.

CHAPTER 13

Mason stared at his phone at his desk, reading a scholarly article on new ways to assess migraines in children, when the familiar chime of an incoming message pulled him out of his medical. Diane's name flashed on the screen, and his heart skipped a beat. His fingers trembled slightly as he opened the message.

Diane: Hey love, I miss you so much. Things are tough here, but I'm getting by. Can't wait to be with you.

Mason's eyes softened as he read her words. Diane was his light in the darkness, the hope he clung to. He could hear her voice in every message and feel the warmth of her presence despite the physical distance. He typed back quickly, his words a lifeline for both of them.

Dr. S.: I miss you too, Diane. How can I help? Do you need more money?"

As soon as he hit send, he felt a pang of guilt. His friends had been relentless in their warnings. "She's a scam, Mason," they'd say. "You're being used." But Mason couldn't believe it. He didn't want to believe it. Diane was real, and she needed him.

The phone buzzed again.

Diane: If you can, it would really help. I'm so close to getting enough for the ticket back home. Just a little more, love. I promise it will be soon.

Mason sighed and opened his banking app. His savings were dwindling, but the thought of Diane finally being with him kept him going. He transferred another $500 and sent her a screenshot of the confirmation.

Diane: Thank you, Mason. I knew I could count on you. You're my everything.

He smiled, but it didn't reach his eyes.

Greg had been particularly vocal about his concerns. They'd had a heated argument just the other night.

"Wake up, Mason!" Greg had shouted, his face red with frustration. "You've sent her thousands of dollars, and you've never even met her in person! She's playing you!"

Mason had slammed his fist on the table. "You don't understand, Greg. She's real. She loves me. And I love her."

Greg had looked at him with a mixture of pity and anger. "You're blinded by your loneliness, Mason. She's manipulating you, and you're letting her."

Mason had stormed out again, refusing to listen. Now, sitting alone in his house, he replayed the argument in his mind. He knew Greg meant well, but he couldn't shake the feeling that Diane was different. She had to be.

The next few weeks passed in a blur. Mason found it harder to concentrate at work, his thoughts constantly drifting to Diane. His phone was always within reach, and his heart leaped with hope every time it buzzed. But the messages were always the same—sweet words of love mixed with requests for money.

One evening, after sending yet another transfer, Mason received a call from Monica. He hesitated before answering, knowing what was coming.

"Mason," she began, her voice gentle but firm. "We need to

talk about Diane."

"Mon, please," he sighed. "Not this again."

"Listen to me," she pleaded. "You're a good man with a big heart, but you're being taken advantage of. I just want you to be happy and safe."

"I am happy," he insisted. "Diane makes me happy."

"Does she?" his friend asked softly. "Or is it the idea of her that makes you happy?"

Mason didn't have an answer. He mumbled an excuse and hung up, feeling the weight of his friends' concern pressing down on him. He wanted to believe in Diane, but the doubts were creeping in, gnawing at the edges of his resolve.

That night, he lay in bed, staring at the ceiling. His mind was a whirlwind of conflicting emotions. He thought about all the money he'd sent, all the promises Diane had made. He wanted so desperately to believe she was real, that their love was real. But what if everyone was right? What if he was just a fool in love with a fantasy? He couldn't be, could he?

The next day, Mason couldn't take it anymore. He decided to confront Diane. He needed answers, needed to know if she was genuine. He typed out a message, his hands shaking.

Dr. S.: Diane, I need to know the truth. Are you really coming back to me? Or is this all just a game to you? I've given you everything I have, and I can't keep going like this. Please, just be honest with me.

He hit send and waited, his heart pounding in his chest. Minutes felt like hours as he stared at his phone, willing it to buzz. When it finally did, he hesitated before opening the message.

Diane: Mason, I can't believe you would doubt me like this. After everything we've been through? I love you, but I can't do this if you don't trust me... Maybe it's better if we just end this...

Panic surged through him.

Dr. S.: No, Diane, please. I'm sorry. I do trust you. I just... I needed to know. I love you too much to lose you.

Diane: Then prove it. Send me the money for the ticket. It's $1000. If you send it, I'll believe you love me, and I'll be on the next flight tomorrow.

Mason felt like he was being torn in two. He knew he couldn't afford to send more money but couldn't bear the thought of losing Diane. And what if all of this griping he was doing was just for her to come back to him tomorrow, and he brought it up for nothing? He transferred another $1,000, draining his account.

Diane: I can't wait to see you. I know you love me. I just needed you to prove it.

Dr. S.: I'll meet you at the airport tomorrow, my love. I can't wait.

Diane: Tomorrow!!!

The next day came, and he was so excited to see her. It took him an hour to drive to the airport at nine am to be there an hour before she arrived just in case her plane was early. Mason had texted Monica and Greg the flight information to prove she was coming home. They both said they were happy for him, but he didn't believe them. Soon. They would see each other so soon. He could hold her any moment now.

He waited outside the terminal with flowers. His hands tightened around the stem as passengers entered the arrivals gate through the glass doors. Stomach filled with butterflies, he scanned the crowd for her face. There was a woman with black hair. There! Walking toward the luggage carousel! Mason sped up toward her, grabbed her shoulder, and turned her toward him.

"Diane?!" Mason bent down to hug her but jolted back at the face that was most certainly not Diane's.

"Oh, um, wrong person. Have a great day!" Mason smiled his most charming smile and scanned the crowd for her. She was nowhere to be found. He pulled out his phone to text her to see if she arrived.

Dr. S.: Where are you? Are you in the bathroom or something? Your flight is here, and I can't find you.

He waited for half an hour with no reply. There was no sign of Diane, and she still hadn't responded. Slumping onto the chair next to the carousel, he figured maybe she just hadn't got off the plane yet, and her phone was still in airplane mode.

Ten texts and fifteen minutes later, his heart skipped a beat at the message that came through. Tears pricked his eyes.

Diane: I'm sorry, my love. The house sale still has not gone through. I won't be home to meet you. I need to be here until the sale goes through.

Mason cried the whole way home. He was humiliated, and the love of his life was still not with him.

Days turned into weeks, and Mason's world continued to unravel. Diane's messages became less frequent, and her excuses more elaborate. He was on edge, snapping at friends and coworkers, not giving his all to his patients, and withdrawing from the people who cared about him. He was a shadow of the man he once was, consumed by his obsession with Diane.

One evening, Greg showed up at his apartment unannounced. Mason tried to ignore the knocking, but Greg was persistent. Reluctantly, he opened the door.

"What do you want?" Mason snapped.

Greg didn't flinch. "We need to talk."

"There's nothing to talk about." Mason moved to close the door, but Greg held it open.

"Yes, there is," Greg insisted, stepping inside. "Mason, look at yourself. You're falling apart. This isn't love—it's a trap."

Mason's anger flared. "Get out, Greg. You don't understand."

"I do understand," Greg said quietly. "More than you know.

My brother was scammed, too, years ago. It took him hitting rock bottom to realize it. I watched him torment himself for weeks. It's the exact same routine. They make you fall in love with them and take you for everything you're worth. They make you doubt yourself and your friends. They isolate you. He- he was a broken man, and I had to watch him go through the exact same thing."

Mason froze, the fight draining out of him. "Chris...?"

Greg nodded. "I know how convincing they can be. But you have to see the truth, Mason. Diane isn't real."

The words hit Mason like a punch to the gut. He sank onto the couch, burying his face in his hands. "I just wanted to be happy," he whispered.

"I know," Greg said, sitting beside him. "But you can't find happiness in a lie."

Mason felt tears burn his eyes. He wanted to believe Greg, to let go of the illusion, but the thought of losing Diane was unbearable.

Greg placed a hand on his shoulder. "We'll get through this together, Mason. You're not alone."

Mason looked up, meeting his friend's gaze. For the first time in months, he felt a glimmer of hope. It warred with his devotion to Diane. She wouldn't be happy about this... but the hope told him that maybe, just maybe, he could find a way out of the darkness.

CHAPTER 14

The next few days passed in a haze. Mason's mind was constantly on Diane and Greg's words. He listened to Greg's plan but said he needed time to consider it. Now, with that conversation in hindsight, Mason just couldn't bring himself to believe Diane was anything but a loving woman in trouble. Finding it hard to focus on anything else, he checked his phone obsessively. The days turned into waiting for her messages. When they came, they were filled with gratitude and love, easing his worries momentarily.

Then, one evening, as he was about to head to bed, his phone buzzed again. He glanced at the screen and saw Diane's name. His nerves flared as he opened the message.

Diane: I hate to ask you this, Mason, but I'm in a really tight spot. I've been trying to save up enough for the plane ticket, but something came up. I need some extra money to cover an unexpected expense.

Mason's blood ran cold.

Dr. S.: Diane, I don't have any more money to send. I've given you everything I have. I gave you money for the flight already. Can't you ask your friends or family?

Diane: They won't help me anymore, and they have nothing more to give. I had to use the money you gave me for the flight on the lawyer's fees. You're the only one I can count on. Please, Mason, I'm begging you. I can't do this without you.

Dr. S.: How much do you need?

Diane: I need about $2,000. I know it's a lot, and I feel terrible asking, but I don't have anyone else to turn to. You're my last hope.

Mason felt like he was suffocating. The room seemed to close in around him as he stared at the screen. He wanted to help her and be the man she believed him to be. But he was running on empty, both financially and emotionally. His hands were trembling as he typed.

Dr. S.: I don't know if I can, Diane... I'm really struggling here. I'm not an ATM. This needs to be the last time, or I'm done.

Diane: Please, Mason. I love you. Don't let me down. I promise this will be the last time. After this, I'll be able to come to you, and we can start our life together.

Mason felt a knot tighten in his chest. He had already sent her so much money; his savings were gone, and he had started sending her almost all of his paychecks. But the thought of Diane struggling, needing him, pulled at his heartstrings.

Dr. S.: Diane, I want to help you, but I'm running low on funds myself. I've already sent you so much.

Diane: I know, and I'm so grateful for everything you've done. This is the last time, I promise. Once I have this, I can finally buy my ticket and be with you. Please, Mason, I need you.

Mason felt tears prick in his eyes. He was trapped, caught between his love for Diane and the harsh reality of his situation. He took a deep breath and typed a single word.

Dr. S.: Ok

As he hit send, a deep sense of dread settled over him. He knew he was in too deep, but he couldn't see a way out. All he could do was hope that Diane's promises were real and that his sacrifices would be worth it in the end.

CHAPTER 15

Mason sat at his computer desk at home. Wasabi was snoozing peacefully on the ground. The glow from the screen cast a soft light over the cluttered surface. His heart raced with anticipation as he reread Diane's last message for the hundredth time.

"I can't believe it, Mason! I finally have everything I need. My flight is booked, and I'll be in your arms in just a few days. I can't wait to start our life together. This is it. We're finally going to be together on Friday night. Love you so much!"

He smiled, feeling a rush of relief and excitement. Everything was finally falling into place. Diane was coming home. He'd spent countless nights imagining this moment, and now it was happening. They had a plan, and it was all going to be ok.

He picked up his phone and dialed Greg's number. He desperately wanted to show the truth to his neighbor and friend. Now he could.

"Hey, Greg. It's Mason," he said when Greg answered. "Can you come over? I have some news."

"Sure thing, Mason. Be there in a few," Greg replied.

A few minutes later, there was a knock on Mason's door. He

opened it to find Greg standing there, a curious look on his face. His friend had been so supportive these last few weeks that Mason couldn't believe Greg had been encouraging him to actually pursue Diane. He felt like the luckiest man in the world.

"Still haven't decorated?" Greg asked as he stepped inside, looking at the house.

"I've been waiting for Diane to come home so she can do it all exactly how she wants!" Mason grinned broadly.

"What's up? Why such a big smile?" Greg looked amused.

Mason could hardly contain his excitement. "Diane's coming home! Her flight is booked, and she'll be here in a few days."

Greg raised an eyebrow, a cautious smile playing on his lips. "That's great news, Mason. I'm happy for you. Did she send you the flight details?"

"Yes, she did," Mason said, handing his phone to Greg. "Look, here's her itinerary. She arrives on Friday evening."

Greg glanced at the details, nodding slowly. "Alright, that's a good sign, I guess. How are you feeling about all this?"

"Excited, nervous, everything all at once," Mason admitted. "I know you don't believe in her, but she's really coming this time! I just want everything to go smoothly."

"It will," Greg said reassuringly. "But remember, it's still important to stay cautious. Make sure everything checks out when she arrives."

Mason nodded. "I will. Thanks for all your help, Greg. I couldn't have gotten through this without you."

"That's what friends are for," Greg said with a smile. "Now, let's make sure you're ready for her arrival. Do you have everything prepared?"

Over the next few days, Mason busied himself with preparations. He cleaned his house from top to bottom, bought fresh flowers, and stocked his fridge with all of Diane's favorite foods. He even took a day off work to get all the feminine supplies she needed.

Friday finally arrived, and Mason could hardly contain his excitement. He spent the day going over every detail, making sure nothing was out of place. As the evening approached, he dressed in his best outfit and headed to the airport, his heart pounding with anticipation.

The drive to the airport felt like it took forever. Mason's mind raced with thoughts of Diane. He imagined their first hug, their first kiss, and the moment they would finally be together without the barrier of a screen between them.

When he arrived at the airport, he checked the flight information board and saw that Diane's flight was on time. He made his way to the arrivals area, eyes scanning the crowd for any sign of her. The minutes ticked by slowly, each one feeling like an eternity.

Finally, he saw her. Diane emerged from the crowd, looking exactly like her pictures. She was even more beautiful in person, and Mason felt his breath catch in his throat. She spotted him and broke into a radiant smile, waving as she made her way toward him.

"Mason!" she called out, her voice filled with excitement. Her voice was smooth as honey and sweet as sugar. It was better than he dreamed.

"Diane!" Mason replied, rushing forward to meet her.

They embraced tightly, the months of longing and uncertainty melting away in that single moment. Mason felt tears prick at his eyes as he held her close, feeling the warmth of her body against his.

"You're really here," he whispered, his voice choked with emotion.

"I am," Diane replied, pulling back slightly to look into his eyes. "I told you we'd be together. And now we are."

Mason kissed her, a gentle, tender kiss that conveyed

all the love and hope he'd held onto for so long. When they finally pulled apart, he took her hand and led her to the truck, their fingers intertwined.

The drive back to Mason's apartment was filled with laughter and conversation. Diane shared stories of her time in DC, and Mason caught her up on everything that had happened in his life. There wasn't much to share on his part since he texted her about it every day, but he was so happy just to hear her voice that he didn't care if he didn't have much to add. It felt natural as if they had known each other for years.

When they arrived at the house, Mason gave her a tour, proudly showing off the preparations he had made. Diane seemed genuinely touched by his efforts, her eyes shining with appreciation.

"It's perfect, Mason," she hugged him tightly. "Thank you for everything."

"I just wanted to make you feel at home," Mason replied, his heart swelling with happiness. Wasabi burst into the living room, and Diane greeted him as if she'd known him since the day he was born. The dog was instantly in love. Mason couldn't have asked for a better meeting.

As they settled into the evening, Mason felt a sense of contentment he hadn't experienced in a long time. They cooked dinner together, laughing and chatting like old friends. It was everything he had hoped for and more.

Later, as they sat on the couch, Diane leaned against him, her head resting on his shoulder. Wasabi laid at their feet, snoring like a freight train. Mason felt a deep sense of peace, knowing they had overcome so much to be together.

"Mason, I have to tell you something," Diane said softly, her voice hesitant.

"What is it?" Mason asked, his heart pounding.

"I want you to know how much I appreciate everything you've done for me," she said, looking up at him with tear-filled eyes. "I know it hasn't been easy, and you've sacrificed a lot. But I'm here now, and I promise to make it all worth it."

"You already have," Mason replied, kissing her forehead. "Having you here is all I ever wanted."

They sat in silence for a while, just enjoying each other's presence. Mason knew there were still challenges ahead, but for now, he was content to bask in the joy of finally being with Diane.

As the night wore on, they made plans for the future, discussing their hopes and dreams. Mason felt a renewed sense of purpose, knowing that he had someone to share his life with.

When they finally went to bed, Mason held Diane close, feeling her warmth and presence beside him. It was the beginning of a new chapter in his life, one filled with love, hope, and the promise of a future together.

As he drifted off to sleep, Mason couldn't help but smile. They had a plan, and it was all going to be ok. Diane was home, and everything was right with the world.

Mason awoke with a start, the sunlight streaming through the window. For a moment, he lay still, basking in the afterglow of the dream. But as reality set in, his heart sank. The bed beside him was empty.

He sat up, rubbing his eyes, and looked around the room. Everything was just as it had been the night before, except for one crucial detail—Diane was nowhere to be found. It had all been a dream, a beautiful, heart-wrenching dream.

Mason's phone buzzed on the nightstand, pulling him further into reality. He picked it up and saw a message from Diane.

Diane: Good morning, love. I hate to ask, but I'm in another tight spot. Can you send me $500 for an emergency? I promise this is the last time. I love you.

Mason stared at the message, the weight of the dream still heavy on his heart. He felt a mix of frustration and despair. He wanted to believe in Diane, but the constant requests for money were more than taking a toll.

He took a deep breath and replied,

Dr. S.: Diane, we need to talk. This can't keep happening. I love you, but we need to find a better way to handle these situations.

As he hit send, he felt a sense of determination. But his resolve quickly crumbled as he thought about the months he had spent waiting, hoping, and believing in her promises. The thousands of dollars he sent were starting to make him suspect he would never get back. The weight of disappointment pressed down on him like a suffocating blanket. He thought it was so real.

The feeling of isolation, of being used, began to erode his willpower. Mason's thoughts grew darker, more desperate. He glanced around his empty house, the walls closing in on him. Tears streamed down his face as he realized just how alone he was.

Mason drove to work in silence. The little shack on the drive seemed to mock him. A broken shell of a building could at least stand firm compared to him.

When he got to the clinic and tried to say hi to Monica, she pulled her lips tight and barely nodded. She didn't say anything and just walked to her desk. Mason was hurt. The last time they spoke, he had yelled at her over a stupid mistake she had made, but it was her fault for making it in the first place.

"Dr. S., do you have a second?" Mason was pulled out of his thoughts by Sherry, who was peaking her head out of an exam room. He smiled and joined her. At least Sherry would be nice to him.

"Dr. S.," Sherry said, "I'm sorry. I have some rough news. I wanted to tell you first before the rest of the clinic finds out. I'm leaving the clinic. I'm going to medical school! I got accepted to OHSU in Portland. Can you believe it?"

Mason's heart sank. Even his medical assistant was abandoning him.

"Congratulations, Sherry," he said shortly, "I'm glad to see your hard work has paid off. Now you can abandon me like everyone else." He sulked out of the room, and Sherry followed.

"Dr. Santiago, wait. I thought you would be happy for me. You always told me I was too smart to be an MA, I don't understand. "

"There's nothing to understand. Go to OHSU. In fact, leave today. I don't need you. We don't have any patients. Don't bother giving your two weeks. You're not fired, but I don't want to hold you back from your dream, so go." Mason knew he was being unreasonable, but he didn't care.

Tears filled in Sherry's eyes, and she said nothing. Mason hated that she didn't even put up a fight for him after all the time they'd been together. Monica rushed to Sherry's side and whispered to her as they walked out the door. Mason knew he would regret letting her leave early, but he could do this without her. He was a neurologist. He was the best. He just needed a couple weeks to himself. The receptionist looked aghast at him when he told her what he wanted her to do.

"Don't look like that. It's not uncommon. I'm the doctor, now do it." He couldn't believe the incompetence of some people.

Monica came in and glared at him. He cut her off before she could open her mouth, "I'm going to take two weeks of vacation. I've already told the receptionist, and she's rescheduling my patients. I'll see you in two weeks. When I get back, I hope you can get over this, whatever it is."

They said nothing to each other as he gathered his things and went home.

CHAPTER 16

Two weeks of vacation was the worst thing he could have done. A week in, and he was the lowest he'd ever felt. The time was filled with doom scrolling and waiting for Diane to reply to him. He'd started to have migraines months before, but they got worse every day. He couldn't even have the lights on in any part of the house. It's like the world hated him.

Even Wasabi seemed to be mad at him. He felt empty and dull, letting the depression take hold. He hadn't been this bad since his father died. Mason started to realize that something needed to change, or he would go crazy. He was already broke. The financial advisor had called Mason the day before and told him his behavior was foolish and that he was falling for a scam. The advisor said he'd given nearly $100k to someone who hadn't had the decency to meet him face to face. Then, the advisor said he was fired from the firm as a client.

Mason had to do whatever he could. Diane had to come home. Now. Laying in total darkness on his bed, he typed out a message to Diane. He could barely look at the screen. Shaking, he hit send.

Dr. S.: Diane, I don't know how much more I can take. I feel like I'm at the end of my rope. If you don't come soon, I don't know what I'll do. I can't live like this anymore.

He hit send, his breath coming in short, ragged gasps. The seconds ticked by slowly, each one amplifying the silence that surrounded him. When Diane's reply finally came, it was cold and dismissive.

Diane: Mason, I'm doing the best I can. You need to be patient. I have my own problems to deal with. I love you and I'll talk to you later.

Mason felt abandoned. The finality of her words cut through him like a knife, and an overwhelming wave of hopelessness washed over him. He stood up, head pounding, pacing the room, his thoughts spiraling into a dark abyss.

Grabbing his phone, he called Greg, his voice shaking as he left a voicemail. "Greg, I need to talk to you. It's urgent. Please call me back."

As he hung up, he stared at the phone, his mind racing. He walked to the bathroom and looked at himself in the mirror. The man staring back at him was a shadow of his former self—tired, broken, and defeated.

In a moment of despair, he reached for the bottle of pills in the medicine cabinet. They were pain meds left over from a dislocated shoulder surgery he'd had not long after he moved here. His hands shook as he fumbled with the cap, tears blurring his vision. The thought of ending the pain, of finding some release from the relentless ache in his heart, seemed like the only way out.

He needed to let Diane know first. She couldn't live not knowing what she'd done to him. He took a photo of the pills and sent it to her.

Diane: What is that? What are you doing?

Dr. S.: This is what it's come to, Diane. This is how far you've driven me.

Diane: Please, don't! Stop right now!

Dr. S.: I'm miserable without you. I can't live without you. I need you here and you refuse to come. How much longer do I have to wait? How much more money do I have to send? When will you ever love me enough to come home? This is what you've driven me to. This is what you've done to me.

Diane: Put those down! I do love you! I am coming home.

Dr. S.: How can I believe you? You've told me everything I want to hear like a sweet little girl for months. How about instead of using Mason the ATM, you take care of yourself for a change. There are resources women have that men don't. How about use some of those before using up a good man and driving him to kill himself.

Diane: I beg of you, stop. You don't know what you're doing.

Dr. S.: Say that you love me.

Diane: I love you! I love you so much. I don't want you to hurt yourself. I know I've asked for a lot, but I never wanted to use you. Please stop. It will just be a little longer and then I'll be there.

Dr. S.: I hope you're happy. When you get here and find my body, be sure to tell my mother I'm sorry and make sure Wasabi is taken care of. I love you. Goodbye.

Mason silenced any notifications from her and stared at his hand. The pills had started to seep their blue color onto his palm. He grabbed the glass of water and filled it to the brim. Gripping the glass too hard, he took a sip of water.

But before he could do anything more, his phone rang. It was Greg. He turned on the speaker phone with his pinky, not trusting himself to move any more than that.

"Mason, what's going on?" Greg's voice was filled with concern.

Mason's grip on the cup loosened. It fell to the floor and shattered, and glass and water sprayed everywhere. He sank to his knees, sobbing uncontrollably. "I can't do this anymore,

Greg. I can't keep going like this. She's never coming. It's all been a lie."

"Stay where you are," Greg said firmly. "I'm coming over right now." Glass started to cut his bare feet, and the blood mixed with the water on the floor. His tears wouldn't end. The pills were half on the floor and half in his hand.

Within minutes, Greg was at Mason's house, pulling him into a tight embrace. "We're going to get through this," Greg said softly. "You're not alone. We're going to find a way to get you the help you need."

Mason clung to Greg, feeling the first glimmer of hope he'd had in months. As the weight of his despair began to lift, he knew that he had to face the truth about Diane, no matter how painful it might be.

Greg gently guided Mason into the room and elevated his feet. Greg cleaned the wounds and the mess on the floor. He flushed away the pain meds and spent the rest of the day with Mason. Greg called Monica, who rushed over.

They spent the day monitoring him while he slept. They removed any possible thing he could hurt himself with. Not once did they leave his side.

The next morning, Mason woke to find them still there. Monica made him breakfast, and they ate silently in the dining room. Wasabi stuck like glue to Mason's leg, whining softly at the bandages on his feet.

Mason looked to his friends and said the words he'd not said in a long time.

"I'm sorry." They spent the day with him silently until he was ready to talk.

"What do I do now?" Mason asked sheepishly.

Monica and Greg smiled at him. They had a plan, and it was all going to be ok. Not the plan he had dreamed of with Diane, but a new one that involved rebuilding his life, finding strength in the support of his friends, and learning to believe in himself again.

CHAPTER 17

Mason sat in his house, the remnants of his latest exchange with Diane lingering in the air. He looked at all her messages from the night before. She seemed truly panicked. He had texted her right before he fell asleep that he didn't go through with it. That he needed some space. She responded with what seemed to be genuine relief, but who knew if she was just glad her living ATM was alive. Thankfully, Diane had given him the space he needed, but he knew it wouldn't last long.

The oppressive weight of her constant demands for money and the heart-wrenching disappointment of their never-materializing reunion had taken a toll on him. The dark thoughts that had clouded his mind the previous night were a stark reminder of how far he had sunk. But now, a new resolve began to form in the clear light of day.

Mason's conversations with Monica and Greg proved that Mason couldn't keep living like this. They finally showed him that he couldn't keep giving pieces of himself away, hoping for a love that seemed perpetually just out of reach. Mason knew he had to change something and that something was within him. It was sour and hard for him to accept. He didn't want to face the truth, but he had to.

Monica and Greg sat at the table, waiting for him patiently, silently encouraging him. He knew what he had to do. As he gathered the courage to end things, his phone buzzed. It was a message from Diane.

Diane: Mason, please. I need you. My situation is getting worse and I don't know what to do without you. If you love me, you'll help me.

Mason felt the familiar pang of guilt and worry. He couldn't keep falling into this trap. Taking a deep breath, he started typing his response. As he typed, he spoke out loud for Monica and Greg to hear.

Dr. S.: Diane, I can't keep sending you money. I've been patient and supportive, but this isn't healthy for me anymore. I need to focus on my own well-being.

Almost immediately, her reply came through.

"She responded, what do I say?" Monica and Greg came to stand over his shoulder and read Diane's words.

Diane: How can you say that? After everything we've been through? You promised you'd be there for me. If you really loved me, you'd understand how much I need you right now. Are you just going to abandon me when I need you the most?

Mason's resolve wavered for a moment. Could he seriously let her go?

"Diane's words are laced with manipulation, each sentence designed to tug at your heartstrings and guilt you into compliance," Greg put a hand on his shoulder and reminded his friend.

"This is what scammers do, Mason," Monica agreed, "You've got to be strong. You have to take care of yourself and be responsible for your actions."

He closed his eyes and took a deep breath, trying to steady himself. He had to stand firm.

Dr. S.: I do love you, Diane. But this isn't about love

anymore. It's about my mental health. I've given so much, and I can't keep doing this.

Diane: But I love you. Do you have that Monica talking to you again? She's just jealous of us, remember? I need you to trust me. I need you. I'll be with you so soon.

Mason couldn't breathe. He hadn't told Monica he'd spoken about her with Diane. He looked to see the hurt in her face. She stepped away but didn't leave. She just silently looked at him, challenging him to do the right thing.

Dr. S.: Yes, I have been, but she's helped me to see the truth. What we have isn't real, Diane. If you aren't a scammer, you're a terrible friend and lover. I've given and given and given and received nothing in return.

Her response was swift and biting.

Diane: So that's it? You're just going to accuse me of horrible things and throw me away? Fine. Maybe I was wrong about you. Maybe you don't care about me at all. I should have known better than to trust you.

Mason's hands trembled as he read her message. Her words hurt, but he could see that Greg was right. She was trying to manipulate him. He had to stay strong. He had to protect himself.

"You know what you need to do, Mason," Greg encouraged.

Dr. S.: No, Diane. This isn't about throwing you away. It's about setting boundaries. I can't keep sacrificing my well-being.

The phone was silent for a moment, then buzzed again.

Diane: Mason, please. I'm begging you. Just one last time. I swear, after this, everything will be fine. I just need $500 to get through this emergency. Please. We'll be together, and I'll make you so happy.

The desperation in her message was palpable, but Mason recognized it for what it was. "It's her last-ditch effort to control me. I know if I give in now, it will never end. I'll be stuck in this cycle forever." Mason stared at the phone, the weight of what he'd done crashing down on him.

"You've got this, Mason," Greg said. Monica nodded. With a deep breath, he typed his final response.

Dr. S.: Diane. I can't help you anymore. I hope you find a way through this, but I need to take care of myself now. Unless you're going to pay me all the money back right now, I will never trust you again. I'm done with this messed up relationship. Goodbye.

He hit send, blocked her number, and immediately felt a weight lift from his shoulders. He had done it. He had stood up for himself. The fear and guilt still lingered, but so did a sense of relief and newfound strength.

He stood up and walked to the window, looking at the world beyond. For too long, he had let his life revolve around someone who was never really there for him. He sacrificed his happiness, self-respect, and financial stability for a relationship that existed only in the digital ether. It was time to reclaim his life.

"Well done, friend," Greg wrapped him in a bear hug. Their eyes pricked with tears.

"I'm happy for you," Monica said. Mason went to hug her, but she backed up, keeping her distance. She walked toward the door and Mason followed. "After what you've said and done, I'm not quite ready to reconcile. I need time. I'm glad you came to your senses and wish you the best. I'll see you at work when you get back. If you need help, please call 911. Greg is going to stay with you and keep an eye on you until he feels you're in the clear."

"Thank you," Mason said as he held open the door for her.

Mason turned to face Greg, and a sad smile was on Mason's face. Greg said, "How about pizza?"

"No, I'm sick of pizza. Want to cook something?"

CHAPTER 18

The next day, Mason spent resting and reflecting. He and Greg hadn't said much to each other, but there was a sense of clear air. He felt like he could finally take a deep breath. The days passed quietly, and Greg felt Mason was ok to be left alone after a few days. Mason took some more time off work. He wanted to figure out some things before he went back to taking care of people.

He decided it was time to go shopping. It was time to make the place his own. He spent the day throwing away anything he ever bought for Diane and replacing them with things that made him happy. Mason felt lighter than he had in months, but something was still off.

The day before Mason returned to work, he was determined to act. Mason grabbed a notebook and began to write. He listed the things he had neglected, the hobbies and passions he had abandoned to pursue a dream that had turned into a nightmare. He wrote about his love for caring for people, the joy he found in working, and the friends he had lost touch with over the years. Each word was a step towards rebuilding his identity.

Next, he listed the people he needed to prepare relationships with Monica, Sherry, and Greg.

The first person he called was Greg. "Hey, Greg. It's Mason. Can we meet up? I need to talk."

"Of course," Greg replied without hesitation. "I'll be over this afternoon when I get off work."

Mason felt a jolt of gratitude. Greg had been there through it all, a steadfast friend who had never judged him.

When Greg arrived at Mason's house that afternoon, he was greeted with a warm smile and a strong hug. "Come on in," Mason said, leading him to the living room.

"Nice change of scenery you got here," Greg admired the room.

"I figured it was time to stop living like this was a temporary place," Mason shrugged.

They sat down, and Mason took a deep breath. "Thank you so much for everything you've done. I couldn't have done it without you. I wouldn't be here without you."

Greg nodded, his expression serious. "I'm proud of you, Mason. That took a lot of courage."

"It did," Mason admitted. "But it also made me realize how much I've lost touch with myself. I've been so focused on trying to make her happy that I forgot about my own happiness."

Greg leaned forward and his eyes filled with understanding. "You have so much to offer, Mason. You're a great friend, a talented physician, and an amazing person. You've lost sight of those things along the way. It's time you start getting back to yourself."

Mason felt tears welling up, but they were tears of relief and recognition. "I want to get back to the things I love. I want to reconnect with old friends and make new ones. I want to live my life for me."

"That's the spirit," Greg said, clapping him on the shoulder. "And you don't have to do it alone. I'm here for you, and so are the people who care about you."

Mason spent the rest of the afternoon with Greg, talking and making plans. They scheduled a hiking trip for the weekend, something Mason hadn't done in ages. They also talked about joining a local trivia club, where Mason could spend the Wednesday evenings getting to be a nerd.

As Mason shut the door behind Greg, Mason felt a sense of optimism he hadn't felt in a long time. Mason decided to go for a walk. He hadn't been out in his own neighborhood in a while. The town around him seemed brighter, more vibrant. He went to a park and sat on a bench. Mason sat and watched people pass by. Each person was absorbed in their own life, and he couldn't help but be curious about them. For the first time in a long time, he felt like he was part of that world again.

He pulled out his phone and scrolled through his contacts, finding numbers he hadn't dialed in months. "Hey, Shelly. It's Mason. I need to talk to you."

Shelly and he had a nice, long talk. He promised a huge going away party and told her he was proud of her.

"Thanks, Doc," he could hear Shelly's smile through the phone.

"Please, call me Mason. Can't wait to see what you do for the world."

The next call was to Monica. Mason stared at her number for a long time. He'd said such horrible things. Would she be willing to talk to him? Would she even want to keep working with him after this? He held his breath as he dialed.

When she picked up, "Hello, Mason," her voice was distant and professional. Swallowing the lump in his throat, Mason prayed this would work.

"You deserve the best friend and coworker," he spit out so quickly that even he could barely understand himself.

"Huh? What are you talking about?" Monica sounded tired.

"I promise to earn your trust back. I want to be friends again. I miss you." Monica didn't say anything for a moment.

"I told you it would take time, Mason." Monica's tone was distant as if she didn't want to have this conversation. He didn't blame her.

"I'm willing to give it all the time you need. I just wanted you to know I'm grateful for you and willing to do what it takes to earn your forgiveness. I won't bug you anymore. I just wanted to let you know." The line stayed quiet save for Monica's breathing. He wasn't sure what else to do.

"I'll see you tomorrow, Mason."

"See you tomorrow."

He hung up the phone and sighed. The walk back to his house was quiet, filled with his thoughts. Maybe he would bring in a special treat for the clinic. It wasn't much, but it was a start.

As Mason sat on his couch that evening, he reflected on the past few weeks. He had stood up for himself and realized his self-worth. He had taken the first steps towards reclaiming his life, and it felt good. Mason had also started to repair things with the people he cared for.

He sighed contentedly as Wasabi jumped up on his lap. There would be challenges ahead, but he felt equipped to face them for the first time in a long time.

Mason smiled to himself, a sense of peace settling over him. His relationship with Diane was no longer his definition. He was Mason, a person of value and worth, and he was ready to embrace whatever the future held.

Then, the phone lit up with a message from Elite Pursuit.

www.ingramcontent.com/pod-product-compliance
Lightning Source LLC
Chambersburg PA
CBHW031042110426
42740CB00046B/654